T0283552

THE
INNOVATIVE
SELLER

Jake Dunlap

THE INNOVATIVE SELLER

Keeping Pace in an AI and Customer-Centric World

WILEY

For general information on our other products and services or for technical support, please contact our Customer Care Department within the United States at (800) 762-2974, outside the United States at (317) 572-3993 or fax (317) 572-4002.

Wiley also publishes its books in a variety of electronic formats. Some content that appears in print may not be available in electronic formats. For more information about Wiley products, visit our web site at www.wiley.com.

Library of Congress Cataloging-in-Publication Data is Available:

ISBN 9781394180240 (Cloth)
ISBN 9781394180257 (ePub)
ISBN 9781394180264 (ePDF)

Cover image(s): © vika_k/Adobe Stock
Cover design: Wiley

SKY10067995_022224

Dedicated to you, the reader, who looks to revolutionize the way we think about sales.

Contents

Acknowledgments

My family,

To my wife and immediate and extended family, words can't express the depth of my gratitude for your support. To my wife, your selflessness and strength have let me pursue my dreams for the last decade. Your sacrifices have not gone unnoticed, and your belief in my vision has been the #1 reason for my success. To my children, your smiles are my greatest motivator, and your understanding means the world to me. Thank you for the countless ways you uplift, inspire, and stand by me. To my parents, Jane, Tom, and Jeff, thank you for all the support over the years. Your hard work and example never went unnoticed and helped to shape the person I am today.

All the people at Skaled,

To the incredible team of professionals at Skaled, your dedication has been the driving force behind our vision to create the future of sales. Your commitment to excellence and the collaborative spirit you bring to our workplace have been pivotal in shaping the future of sales. Each of you has contributed uniquely, offering innovative ideas, tireless energy, and unwavering support as we navigate the evolving landscape of our industry. Your collective talents and insights have not only propelled our company forward but have also set new standards in sales excellence. To Matt Lopez, your dedication and loyalty over the years have truly made all this possible. Without your support, who knows if I would be where I am today. I am profoundly thankful for your contributions and proud to stand alongside all the Skalers as we continue to redefine the horizons of what we can achieve together.

To the vibrant community of followers on LinkedIn,

YouTube, and other social media platforms—thank you. Whether you've been with me since my first tentative post or joined somewhere along the journey, your support has been a key ingredient in transforming my lone voice into a chorus of shared learning and growth. Here's to you, the unseen yet ever-present comrades in my online adventure!

Sales leaders,

I would like to extend my heartfelt gratitude to the myriad sales leaders and influencers whose wisdom and insights have been a beacon of guidance throughout my career. Bryan Ross taught me in my first role the value of reading and treating sales truly as a profession. Evan Ross taught me the value of the sales process and taking control of your career. To professionals such as Kevin Dorsey, John Barrows, Scott Lease, Chris Walker, and many others, your innovative strategies, profound wisdom, and relentless passion for excellence have not only shaped the landscape of revenue strategies but have also immeasurably enriched my professional journey.

Clients over the years,

In this journey of continuous growth and learning, our most sincere appreciation is reserved for you, our partners and clients. Your openness to innovation and willingness to embrace new strategies have been the cornerstone of our shared success. You have not only entrusted us with your business challenges but have also been active participants in the pioneering spirit that drives progress. The collaborative environment you've fostered has allowed us to test and refine cutting-edge methodologies, paving new paths forward in the sales domain. To Greg Stewart, your partnership and mentorship have been critical to my success, and I'm very fortunate to call you a friend and mentor today. We are deeply thankful for your partnership, which has been fundamental to our mission and a testament to the power of collective ambition and trust.

The sales leaders and CEOs who fired me,

I extend a heartfelt thank-you to the distinguished league of sales leaders and CEOs who, at one time or another, decided my talents were best appreciated elsewhere. Your gift of "career redirection" proved to be an unexpected catalyst for growth, and for that, I am ironically grateful. Each pink slip was a road sign toward a path less traveled, a nudge (or shove) toward uncharted territories where I found success on my own terms. Cheers to you all for the unintended pushes forward.

About the Author

Jake Dunlap is the industry-leading CEO on Modern Sales and Revenue Trends. As the CEO of Skaled Consulting, he helps CEOs, PE, and VC firms along with VPs of sales break down the complexities of scaling quickly to increase sales and scale effectively. Jake has worked with thousands of top revenue leaders and teams globally, such as Microsoft, Splunk, NFL, and NBA, to modernize their sales organizations, driving hundreds of millions of dollars in new revenue. He was recognized internationally by LinkedIn as the only CEO in the latest Top Voices for Sales list in 2023, and his insights have been featured in national media outlets such as the *New York Times*, *Forbes*, and *Huffington Post* and many leading podcasts, including the Gary Vee Audio Experience.

1

Innovation Isn't Hard, Breaking Old Habits Is

EVERY DAY WE see the success stories of visionaries who see a big trend, do something about it, and it completely changes the way we live. These people appear to have seen something that everyone else missed. Then we see the other side, where companies stick with the status quo as their businesses are slowly eroded by shifts in consumer behavior. Years later, it is easy to look back and wonder how so many companies missed that boat one way or the other.

Shellye Archambeau—who was on my podcast in 2021 and currently serves on the boards of several prominent companies, including Verizon, Nordstrom, Roper Technologies, and Okta—told a story about a company some of you may know, Blockbuster, and another company we all know, Netflix. Shellye was the president of Blockbuster's e-commerce division in 1999, and she and the CEO at the time met with a young entrepreneur, Reed Hastings, in 2000. This former Peace Corps member and Stanford grad came to Blockbuster with an idea. Netflix had already launched their mail delivery DVD service and had some initial traction. Blockbuster was still the big player in the movie rental business, with their extensive web of branches that accounted for over 9,000 stores globally with declared revenue of around $5.9 billion in 2004. His idea was simple: you have all these people coming to stores to rent. What if they could access movies in their homes without coming to the location? Reed proposed a simple solution to give Blockbuster the best of all worlds—let's combine blockbuster.com and Netflix. This would give Blockbuster three convenient ways, store, direct to home, and online, to meet buyers where they wanted to buy and consume movies.

Today this answer might seem fairly obvious. Of course, people would like to have the option to not travel to a store where the movie you want might not even be available, versus getting something mailed to your house in a day guaranteed or streamed online.

So what would you choose when the Internet was just taking shape and technology was becoming a part of everyday life? Looking back, the answer is clear, but when you are the biggest company in a sector and your business model is working, how tough would it be to make this call? This was one of those pivotal moments in time, when a visionary, in this case Reed Hastings, saw where consumer trends were heading and took the idea to the largest company in the space. He offered the CEO a chance to not only continue to dominate the market but also open up completely new ways to do business and engage customers in new ways.

The CEO said no.

He turned down Reed Hastings and said he would stick with the model that had worked for them since 1985. By the time they saw the light, it was too late. The company lost $984 million despite $5.9 billion in revenue. They tried to mimic the model by introducing a mail delivery service in 2004, but by that time, Netflix had already crossed 2.48 million active subscribers. By 2010, Blockbuster declared bankruptcy following a loss of just under $1 billion, while Netflix reached 18.26 million subscribers.

There were thousands of companies that went out of business when the shifts in consumer behavior and the Internet took over the way we purchase. Companies that didn't adapt to changes in consumer behaviors by adapting their business model to focus on speed of purchase and convenience paid the price.

Moving at Light Speed

The last 15 years have been fun and fast. Since that time, it's clear that innovations that focus on speed and convenience are winning.

Can you name what year each of these services became a part of our everyday life:

- Amazon Prime
- Streaming services
- Food delivery (at scale)
- Uber/ride sharing

All of these were either launched in the last 15 years or became a part of our daily lives during that period.

Previously food delivery meant pizza, shopping meant going to the mall or mail order, and let's not forget about cabs and taxis. Most people under the age of 30 have probably never set foot in one . . . it was an experience. Speed and convenience prior to these innovations were based on the way the company wanted you to buy and their terms. You had to come in, talk to a person, and deal with the stock that was available or wait for someone to drive by and pick you up—all on their terms.

Now, I buy things on Amazon daily/weekly. At least three or four times a month, I pick a product that gets to my house faster over the original product I wanted. Sometimes it's even more expensive, so I'm picking an inferior product just so I can get the value from it faster. I do the same thing for my family on DoorDash, often picking the faster option over what we might really want for lunch or dinner.

I don't think I'm alone here. How many of you can relate?

All of these modern conveniences are totally based on the speed of the purchase. The speed that we are able to consume whatever it is we buy continues to get closer and closer to real time. Convenience and speed are nearly the same thing today. Recent McKinsey & Company research asserts that emerging patterns of consumer demands are reshaping last-mile delivery where 23% of the consumers were willing to pay more to get same-day delivery and around 60% now indicate an expectation of even faster deliveries using drones and related technologies.

Customers Are More Savvy

Sure, many of these purchases are considered more transactional in nature, but how have the biggest purchases in our lives evolved?

Consider home buying, one of the largest purchases many people make in their lifetime. Nearly all buyers used online tools in the search process at 96%. 43% of buyers first looked online for properties, while only 18% first contacted a real estate agent. 87% of people end up working with a realtor, but the buyer did the research and got all the way down the funnel all on their own. In fact, 8% of people would have preferred not to work with a real estate agent but felt they had to. For even the biggest purchases, people are completely changing the way they buy. They want to gather information, learn on their own, and then possibly get a human involved.

Car buying, vacations, expensive furniture, and even picking the right college—the major decisions are nearly all started online. The consumer evaluates options quickly, looks at various sites, talks to friends, and then either completes the entire purchase online or does the research and then moves to a human interaction. Just 15 years ago, people made nearly all of these purchases with the help of a person first or early in the process and expected it to take time to make the right decision. Now we do all of these activities in a matter of hours on our own schedules. The way we buy everything—small and big—will continue to get faster, and the buying experience will continue to be more tailored to our individual buying habits to suit the way we want to buy.

Business-to-Business Sales Today

When I look at today's business-to-business (B2B) sales process, I can't help but think of Blockbuster, the mall, and the taxi. Each of these had one way to buy, completely dictated by the company's terms and how they wanted to sell or deliver services. Many B2B sales teams consistently exhibit the same behavior by having one sales process for everyone, regardless of how educated or quickly the buyer wants to make a decision. They are offering a retail-only experience, where people have to go through the same process regardless of who or where they are in the buying process.

As our consumer purchasing behavior has been revolutionized, the B2B process must innovate to keep pace. Expecting a buyer to be satisfied by a clunky process entirely dependent on a sales rep providing knowledge is unsustainable, when we compare it to how quickly our consumer buying behavior has evolved. B2B buyers are coming to companies expecting a B2C experience, but instead they are getting Blockbuster. Let's look at when the most popular sales methodologies were developed:

- 1967 Sandler Selling System
- 1978 Miller-Heiman, Strategic Planning
- 1988 Solution Selling (SPI)
- 1988 SPIN Selling
- 1991 Value Selling (as ValueVision Associates)
- 1993 Customer-Centric Selling
- 2002 RAIN Selling
- 2005 Baseline Selling
- 2011 The Challenger Sale

MEDDIC is another one that I see many companies use, and it was invented in 1996. A majority of sales organizations are using techniques and implementing sales processes that were built before the Internet or before all of the innovation I just mentioned.

This disruption is further compounded by *Generative AI* such as ChatGPT, Bard, and many others. *Generative AI* refers to a subset of artificial intelligence that is designed to create new, original content, ranging from text and images to music and more. Unlike traditional AI systems that analyze and interpret data, generative models actively produce content, often leveraging deep learning techniques. This ability to generate amazing outputs makes *Generative AI* distinct, enabling applications such as art creation, sales messaging, and realistic simulation environments, which I discuss in detail later.

These tools are further disrupting the way buyers access information and demand access to solutions. Today, right now, buyers are going to these tools, dropping in your website and two or three of your competitors, and asking generative tools how you are different compared to your competitors, giving them their key criteria and then asking ChatGPT to tell them the best solution. They no longer need to research 30, 40, or 50 hours to get a sense for what a product can do and how it can help. They can get these answers in seconds, and they come to calls more prepared than you might imagine.

Buyers are coming to sales calls with a growing level of understanding and an expectation that the salesperson and the organization can meet them where they are. The "rent in store only option" is not working. The world has evolved and continues to evolve at a pace where it is time now for B2B sales to catch up.

Making B2B Sales Innovative

We can all see the way people buy is shifting, but many senior sales leaders are still consistently building from old frameworks and methodologies that just don't fit how buyers want to buy. It's shocking to think that the most popular sales methodologies being used by B2B sales teams were invented 20–30 years ago. Instead of evolving with technology, we have tried to fit technology into these old, outdated modalities.

The time to innovate is now. This book gives you, as a CEO, sales leader, or B2B salesperson, the tactical road map to evolve, rebuild, retrofit, and update the way you go to market and interact with customers. This book teaches you how to create a process that is both repeatable and meets the modern buyer where they are today.

I've spent the last 10 years leading thousands of B2B companies through these changes and have developed a framework that easily meets buyers where they are. It may seem like a big leap for your organization to take, but the central theme of this book is a simple one: *innovation isn't hard, breaking old habits is.*

Key Takeaways

- **The importance of speed and convenience:** Over the past 15 years, innovations that prioritize speed and convenience have dominated markets. Companies such as Amazon streaming services, food delivery platforms, and ride-sharing services have become integral parts of our daily lives. Consumers now prioritize speed, even at the expense of product quality or preference.

- **B2B sales need to evolve:** The traditional B2B sales process is outdated, with many companies still relying on old frameworks and methodologies. Modern B2B buyers expect a consumer-like experience, with quick access to information and solutions. *Generative AI* tools, such as ChatGPT and Bard, are further disrupting the sales landscape by providing instant answers and insights.

Further Reading

Chhabria, Ashwin, "The Rise of Netflix and the Fall of Blockbuster," Medium, March 23, 2017, https://scashwin .medium.com/the-rise-of-netflix-and-the-fall-of-blockbuster-29e5457339b7.

Davis, Todd, and John Higgins, "A Blockbuster Failure: How an Outdated Business Model Destroyed a Giant," Chapter 11 Bankruptcy Case Studies, University of Tennessee College of Law, 2013, https://ir.law.utk.edu/cgi/viewcon tent.cgi?article=1010&context=utk_studlawbankruptcy.

Dean, Brian, "Netflix Subscriber and Growth Statistics: How Many People Watch Netflix in 2023," Backlinko, March 27, 2023, https://backlinko.com/netflix-users.

"Frequency of Internet Use for Home Searching in the United States in 2022, by Age Group," Statista, August 3, 2023, https://www.statista.com/statistics/507513/frequency-of-internet-use-for-home-searching-usa-by-age-group/.

Giovanetti, Erika, "97% of Buyers Shop for Houses Online, Report Finds: Tips for Buying a Home in the Digital Age," Fox Business, October 7, 2021, https://www.foxbusiness.com/personal-finance/shopping-for-houses-online-tips-for-buying.

"Highlights from the Profile of Home Buyers and Sellers," National Association of Realtors, n.d., https://www.nar.realtor/research-and-statistics/research-reports/highlights-from-the-profile-of-home-buyers-and-sellers.

Huddleston Jr., Tom, "Netflix Didn't Kill Blockbuster—How Netflix Almost Lost the Movie Rental Wars," CNBC, September 22, 2020, https://www.cnbc.com/2020/09/22/how-netflix-almost-lost-the-movie-rental-wars-to-blockbuster.html.

Joerss, Martin, Florian Neuhaus, and Jürgen Schröder, "How Customer Demands Are Reshaping Last-Mile Delivery," McKinsey & Company, October 2016, https://www.mckinsey.com/~/media/McKinsey/Industries/Travel%20Logistics%20and%20Infrastructure/Our%20Insights/How%20customer%20demands%20are%20reshaping%20last%20mile%20delivery/How-customer-demands-are-reshaping-last-mile-delivery.pdf.

Sloan, Molly, "Netflix vs. Blockbuster—3 Key Takeaways," Drift, June 1, 2020, https://www.drift.com/blog/netflix-vs-blockbuster/.

2

Introducing the 4 Cs of Modern Sales Transformation

I TALK TO hundreds of CEOs and VPs of sales every year. What is holding many back from changing is the thought of going against what made them successful for decades. Despite the fact that 68% of salespeople say that their role has permanently changed due to the shifts in the sales landscape, asking a leader who took a company public or scaled a company to a billion in revenue to pivot to a new model feels like a nearly impossible task. Ask any seller who has seen success in their career if they would like to change what's made them successful—you are going to get quite a bit of hesitancy.

I get it. As a lifelong seller and sales leader, I would be a bit nervous reading a book that tells me if I don't adapt, I might end up like Blockbuster. The good news is that from my work with thousands of companies, I've honed the practice of making change management applicable and tactical, so even the most seasoned leader and salesperson can make this adaptation quickly. Interestingly, 52% of sales leaders believe that their teams need to improve their adaptability skills. I use the word *adaptation* very specifically because this is all that is required. You don't need to change everything up or throw everything out the window to make your B2B selling process innovative. In fact, most organizations and sellers already have the building blocks to get there. In order to make this adaptation easier, I've honed all of my work and experience down to four simple principles call the 4Cs. Over the course of this book we will review the key concepts in the principle, understand the 3 pillars that make up each principle, and give you the tactical roadmap to move from your current to ideal state. Most are already doing pieces of the puzzle, and the 4 Cs will really help you pull those pieces together in an actual framework that is easy to deploy and execute. Let's walk through the 4 Cs now.

The 4 Cs of Innovative Selling

I've distilled the necessary steps for innovation in sales organizations down to what I call the 4 Cs:

- Commitment to technology and AI proficiency
- Current go-to-market (GTM) strategy
- Customized sales journey
- Consistent performance optimization

The 4 Cs of Innovative Selling is a framework to help break old habits that aren't working anyway and rebuild sales organizations and sales skills/processes, all to meet the changes in consumer behavior and rise of AI. Each section in the chapters that follow maps to one of these principles. The chapters that follow are arranged just like a typical sale, from how to generate more meetings through closing the deal. This makes it easier for you to map innovations to your current process for easy adaptation.

These pillars are embedded in the chapters, and each principle is actionable.

These four principles can take any company from its current state to innovation in a matter of weeks/months, and each principle is critical to making this a reality. Each principle has three tactical pillars that anyone can focus on individually to master. These principles are dependent on each other, and while implementing just one principle will be an immediate improvement to your current process or team, without the others, you may not unlock the innovation you are hoping for. So don't jump ahead too soon.

With that said, if you want a few tips on one specific principle so you can close a deal this month, feel free to skip ahead to that chapter. Just be sure to come back to the process. Without further ado, let's talk through the principles and pillars of each at a high level.

Principle One: Commitment to Technology and AI Proficiency

Principle one is a commitment to technology and AI proficiency (CTAP) which will be critical to building and scaling amazing sales organizations as technology today. Technology today will transform tomorrow's teams. A staggering 63% of sales organizations are increasing their technology investments to stay competitive. However, 74% of sales professionals say they spend too much time on tasks, which detracts from their selling time. Right now, many sales leaders and teams are questioning these big investments because the productivity gains aren't quite what was promised. The good news is that it's fixable. Here are the pillars that will help you get there:

Here are the pillars, which will discuss each one in Chapter 3, that will help you get there.

- Engineering technology to match customer behavior changes
- Ensuring technology and process are intertwined
- Habits to stay at the forefront

I addressed the first pillar in Chapter 1. So congratulations, you already have an idea about one of the 12 pillars. Most people find that this pillar is the easiest to understand because everyone can completely relate to it in their everyday lives.

The other two pillars tackle head-on the poor implementation of many process and technology changes, along with new habits for organizations to adopt to continue this process in perpetuity. This principle walks you through the importance of looking at technology and process changes as one. Technologies are often implemented based on the latest trend, and then new methodologies are implemented, many 20–30 years old, to fix process changes that don't actually solve the real issues for not hitting revenue targets. These two issues lead to poor adoption and lack of buy-in from the sales organization. Throw in *Generative AI*, and things get even more critical. You can no longer outsource your knowledge of these tools to technical teams because the technology should be at the heart of how you build a modern B2B sales organization. With AI, we are seeing productivity gains of 20%–30% overnight by consolidating hundreds of hours of research and learning into minutes and hours. All sellers and sales leaders must have a commitment to staying on top of technology trends

Principle Two: Current Go-to-Market Strategy

Principle two is an adjustment of thinking to how many companies lead marketing and their outbound strategy. We continue to focus on trying to automate more activities versus higher quality of touchpoints. For many, if not all revenue organizations, high volumes of activities as a primary focus will lead to few results. Consider these three pillars that make up excellence at this principle:

- Marketing and lead generation team alignment
- Focus on outcomes and not on volume metrics only
- Hyper-customized touchpoints in outbound

In the latest 2023 report from Skaled Consulting, only 9% of companies were hitting their outbound goals. The volume of outbound B2B continues to grow with over 306 billion emails sent every day. When I said earlier that all of these principles are intertwined, these issues are related to the first principle because it is the lack of understanding of how to use key technologies that has landed many marketing and sales organizations here. Companies began overusing technology to automate emails, with no personalization, and developed a mindset of "If we want something to be scalable, we have to automate it." It's the quantity-over-quality mindset, but as the volume of activities has gone up, the results and performance of teams have gone down.

Many companies have looked to automate GTM activities instead of thinking of ways to automate the mundane so humans can focus on higher-quality, custom activities. Alarmingly, 57% of sales reps expected to miss their quotas in 2023, and it's no wonder when you look at the types of activities we are asking sellers to do. The future of teams is tracking a lower volume of activities and a shift in focusing on results-based KPIs.

Having a current, relevant GTM strategy is critical to every company that is looking to grow. Current strategies utilize technology to automate behind-the-scenes activities, create paths for buyers to learn more without salespeople being involved, and then create scalable ways for salespeople to generate more pipeline. These three pillars address each of these issues. Once you start to see just how intertwined all of the principles of the 4 Cs are, you'll understand why so many organizations are struggling to innovate.

Principle Three: Customized Sales Journey

Principle three is focused on building a sales journey based on how customers want to buy. Most if not all current B2B sales methods are built from the viewpoint of how companies want to sell instead of how people want to buy. Customers want speed and a personalized experience. The pillars for this principle are as follows:

- The customer journey is mapped and optimized for the ideal experience at each step

- Options are included for customers to learn more without calls
- Plans exist to move customers who are high intent to later stages quickly

A majority of this book focuses on this principle, where I go through details on how to build a repeatable process to meet your customers where they are at each step in the process. In fact, customer experience (CX) has been ranked as the number-one priority for businesses, surpassing product and pricing. Companies that invest in CX initiatives can potentially double their revenue.

That same study found a significant 86% of buyers are willing to pay more for a superior customer experience. The more expensive the item, the more customers are willing to pay, with some even willing to pay a premium of up to 13%–18% for luxury services if they receive an excellent customer experience.

If you are a frontline rep, you are going to walk away from this book with a whole new playbook for how to interact with customers, generate more late-stage deals, and by using AI and technology, do it all easier.

Sales leaders can use this as a blueprint for your sales organization to meet customers where they are in their specific journey and close more deals faster. The discussion touches on all of the 4 Cs, because they are critical to the success of this principle, but without getting this one right, it is truly impossible to innovate the sales organization.

We have to have a process that is focused on our customers first and the sales process second to match. According to Salesforce, 84% of buyers are more likely to buy from a salesperson who understands their goals, but 57% say sales reps don't know enough about their industry. This new process of customer-first thinking will help organizations close more deals and build more trusted relationships.

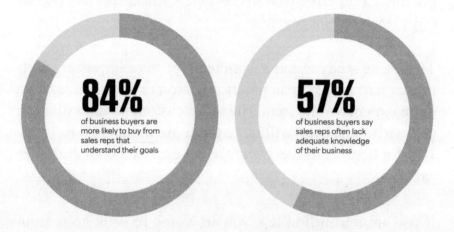

84%
of business buyers are
more likely to buy from
sales reps that
understand their goals

57%
of business buyers say
sales reps often lack
adequate knowledge
of their business

This goal of this sales process is to allow buyers to buy the way that is best for them, yet have salespeople in the loop at key moments throughout the process. To be clear, salespeople are still at the heart of B2B sales, but you still develop new strategies for new buyer behaviors. The process that will win tomorrow is a process focused on customized sales journey and not on a one-size-fits-all methodology.

Principle Four: Consistent Performance Optimization

Principle four is consistent performance optimization. Many B2B sale teams optimize their outbound process every 6–12 months and their sales process every two to three years. This worked when buying was the same for everyone and we didn't have the technology to track outcomes in real time, but we have to optimize more consistently to align to rapidly changing buyer behaviors. The three pillars for this principle are:

- Know what to measure and when.
- Have a mechanism for infusing improvements without disruption.
- Build ways to break the status quo.

An interesting habit of B2B sales is the mindset of big changes or shiny new technologies to fix real sales challenges over smaller, consistent changes regularly. Many salespeople expect these big new playbooks, new methodologies, or latest technologies to fix their sales issues when, in reality, it's the ongoing optimization of a process that leads to optimal results over time. Think about the Netflix and Amazon analogies in the first chapter. These tools constantly analyze personalized choices and provide customized content to customers in real time—the process gets better with time, and quickly.

Another comparison comes from our counterparts in marketing. Marketing teams will put up an ad, see how it performs in a matter of minutes or hours, take it down if it's not working, rewrite, repost, and then follow that process again and again in order to optimize performance. They are pumping hundreds of thousands of data points through a system, quickly seeing results, and then making changes. B2B sales is pumping hundreds of thousands of data points through a process to see what works every day/week/month but aren't optimizing the same way. B2B is running hundreds of demos, hearing customer feedback every month, and then optimizing every two years? This makes no sense in today's modern era.

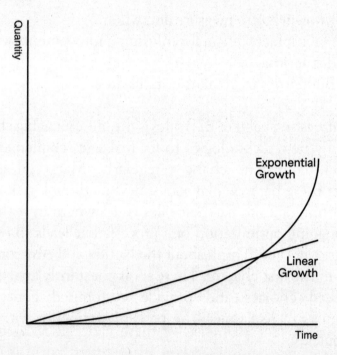

To build this new mindset, you need to establish the most important metrics, find a way to infuse ongoing improvements into the organization without major disruption, and then build in ways to test big new ideas.

Summary

There you have it. The 4 Cs that will help both organizations and individual sellers align to how buyers want to buy. It's time—maybe you've been running the same basic playbook for more than 20 years. If so, the time for innovation is now.

B2B sales has been in need of a new process and operating rhythm for many years now. I'm excited to walk you through this new innovative model, and I'll go deep into the key steps of each of the 4 Cs, which will allow you to enjoy big change quickly in your organization.

Over the next ten chapters, I'll take you through the key steps in the customer journey and how to incorporate the 4 Cs tactically. Additionally, I've tried to make this book an everyday guide that you can come back and consult daily as challenges arise. It can serve as a reference you can use to quickly jump to any key point in the process where you are struggling. Also, make sure you join our Innovative Seller movement at resources.innovativesellerbook.com. We have a growing community of leaders and sales professionals who are applying all of what you are learning now every day.

As mentioned earlier, half of these chapters focus on the third principle, the *customized sales journey*, but it is important to spend time on each of the 4 Cs. Otherwise, you will never enjoy the full benefit and won't be able to fully implement the processes.

The next three chapters go deeper into the commitment to technology and AI proficiency and the necessity to have a current outbound and GTM strategy. You cannot build customized journeys for your customers without technology, and you won't have customers if you can't generate meetings, so these first two principles are critical contention points for every seller or leader reading this book. Let's kick off with the first C, *commitment to technology and AI proficiency*, because the question in many sellers' and leaders' minds is how the hell do we actually integrate technology and process anyway?

Key Takeaways

- **Sales must adapt:** The sales landscape has undergone significant changes, with 68% of salespeople acknowledging a permanent shift in their roles. Despite this, many seasoned leaders are hesitant to adapt due to past successes. A complete overhaul isn't necessary; instead, adaptation is key. Many organizations already possess the foundational elements for innovation.
- **Use the 4 Cs framework for innovative selling:** The 4 Cs are commitment to technology and AI proficiency, current go-to-market (GTM) strategy, customized sales journey, and consistent performance optimization. This framework is designed to break outdated habits and reconstruct sales organizations so they align with evolving consumer behavior and the rise of AI. While each principle is valuable on its own, they are interdependent and most effective when implemented together.
- **Sales must commit to technology and AI proficiency:** Embracing technology is crucial for future sales teams.

A significant 63% of sales organizations are upping their tech investments. The three pillars under this principle are recognizing the changing customer behavior due to technology, understanding the interrelation of technology and process, and cultivating habits to remain updated.

- **Your current go-to-market (GTM) strategy isn't working:** Adjusting the current marketing and outbound strategy is essential. A mere 12% of companies are achieving their outbound goals, despite the surge in outbound B2B activities. The pillars for this principle include aligning marketing and lead generation teams, focusing on outcomes rather than just volume metrics, and emphasizing hyper-customized touchpoints in outbound strategies. A shift from quantity to quality is necessary, as the overreliance on automation and lack of personalization have led to decreased performance.
- **You need a customized sales journey:** Customers today demand swift and personalized experiences. The pillars for this principle are optimizing the customer journey at each step, providing options for customers to learn independently, and having strategies to quickly move high-intent customers through the sales process. Customer experience (CX) is paramount, with studies showing that companies focusing on CX can potentially double their revenue. The goal is to allow buyers to purchase in a manner that suits them, with salespeople playing a pivotal role at crucial junctures.
- **You need consistent performance optimization:** The fourth principle emphasizes the importance of regular and consistent tweaks and changes, rather than

waiting for major overhauls or new technologies to address sales challenges. The pillars for this principle are understanding what metrics to measure and when, having a mechanism to seamlessly integrate improvements, and creating strategies to challenge the status quo. To foster a culture of continuous improvement, it's essential to identify crucial metrics, ensure ongoing enhancements without major disruptions, and test innovative ideas.

Further Reading

Niklas Stattin, "32 Customer Experience Statistics You Need to Know for 2024," SuperOffice, December 1, 2023, https://www.superoffice.com/blog/customer-experience-statistics/.

Kirsch, Katrina, "The Ultimate List of Email Marketing Stats for 2023," HubSpot, December 14, 2023, https://blog.hubspot.com/marketing/email-marketing-stats.

"State of Sales, Fourth Edition," Salesforce, https://www.salesforce.com/content/dam/web/en_sg/www/documents/research/salesforce-state-of-sales-4th-ed.pdf.

"What Are Customer Expectations, and How Have They Changed?" Salesforce, August 2023, https://www.salesforce.com/resources/articles/customer-expectations/?sfdc-redirect=369.

https://www.quotapath.com/blog/sales-teams-miss-quota/).

3

The First C: Commitment to Technology and AI Proficiency: People, Process, and Technology

WE TACKLED PILLAR engineering technology to match customer behavior changes, and it lives in this principle because most of the innovations that drive customer changes were due to advances in technology. In 2020, 54% of sales leaders said sales operations was key to defining strategy, a number that has since increased to 65%. The way we buy as consumers drives innovation, and the speed at which technology is making the impossible possible is staggering. In B2B sales, we need to change the way we embrace this mindset. This chapter tackles the second and third pillars of CTAP (the commitment to technology and AI proficiency), which will tactically help you implement change that incorporates technology and process improvements that will actually stick and show real impact on your revenue.

Knowledge Is Power

When I was fresh out of college, I was fortunate enough to get a job selling tickets for a Major League Baseball team. It was my dream job. I was quickly promoted from group sales to account executive and then to senior account executive, where a counterpart and I built out the inside sales team. It was a really fast 16 months, but there was something funny that happened about 12 months into the role that accelerated my growth faster than my peers'.

Coming from college, I had zero experience with a customer relationship management (CRM) tool, and the training on the tech stack was mediocre at best. I did have experience in Excel and statistics tools from school and understood that for my own performance, the data I put into the system would determine the quality of insights I could get out. I was hungry to learn and read every book I could get about top sales techniques. I also doubled down on harnessing the data on my performance from our CRM because I knew it could make my life easier if I could figure out what was and wasn't working.

Our inbound phone system, where people called in to buy ticket packages from the website, was basic. It was a round-robin system that would skip you if you were on a call. Someone calls in, and then it skips to the next person not on the phone. Pretty basic. After my first season with the team was over, I got curious and turned to our CRM for insights. I had a simple question: Was there a time of day that people were more or less likely to call in that I should be making my calls so I could get more inbound leads? I was already one of the top two sellers in the organization, but I saw a potential opportunity here.

I pulled the historical data from the prior season on all closed won opportunities from that lead source (inbound calls), I pulled the time of the call, and then I exported that data into Excel to create a scatterplot comparing sold deals to the times when people called in. The data was clear. I found that from 11–11:30, 2–2:45, 4–4:30ish, and a few other blocks in the day, no sales were made. Logically it made sense as it was the time when people are most likely to be working.

I took the data and ran with it. For the next two weeks, I sat there in the morning and did all my busy work and then started dialing like a maniac during those windows. The results? I started cleaning up and getting nearly all the inbound calls. As you can imagine, my coworkers got a little upset as I was taking down deal after deal as they dialed away. This is where it gets wild. At the end of the first week,

I showed them the data! I said, "Hey all, check out this pattern I found, and this is why I'm doing it . . . you all should think about it too." What was the result of me sharing this new, helpful information? Nothing—they kept doing their same old habits. Despite the data, despite the results, they kept doing what they were told to do. Eventually, they adjusted the round-robin system, and I made amends with everyone. However, this taught me something early—the salesperson and organizations who knows how to use tools and data will do exponentially better than the average high-performing salesperson and team who doesn't.

Don't Be Afraid to Get Creative with Your Tools

My sales technology obsession and desire to improve my own and my sales team's performance didn't end there. When I was the Vice President of Sales at Glassdoor in 2011, I purchased and implemented Marketo, which is a tool used by marketers in nearly all use cases. It lets marketers create fairly sophisticated email campaigns. The twist was that I bought this for the sales team, not for marketing. I still remember the Marketo rep being confused, but I went ahead with it because as soon as I saw a demo, I immediately saw the impact it could have on the team. It gave my team the ability to build complex sequences, which allowed them to set two to three times more meetings than a normal seller without sacrificing quality. We were able to leverage persona and proprietary Glassdoor data we had on company pages to create world-class outbound sequences. The results were real—we went from nearly $0 monthly

(continued)

> recurring revenue when I started to $1 million in less than 16 months. By leveraging technology and integrating it with a great process, we were able to quickly surpass other teams selling into the same buyer.

My obsession with the integration of technology and improvements to solve challenges comes from the results I've seen over the years that have led to multibillion-dollar exits and valuations from the companies I've worked for and with. So when I say that technology and process can be integrated, I'm speaking from experience.

Plus, when you dig deep enough, you can find some interesting patterns that can truly break the system and skyrocket results (just try not to anger your coworkers in the process).

Removing the Technology Stigma

If my results are so great, why do only 37% of sales professionals strongly agree that their organization fully utilizes their tech, and why are 94% of organizations evaluating their tech stack in the next 12 months?

History is the answer. When most salespeople, and sales leaders for that matter, hear the words "sales" and "technology" in the same sentence, their eyes immediately glaze over. This sentiment is improving with new sales technologies that are slightly easier to use, but for many people with more than a few years of experience, the scar tissue is already there. I can relate to this mindset, as I had it myself at times.

We've been yelled at for not putting data in the CRM (which we never go back and look at anyway). We've struggled to build reports or dashboards that accurately analyze sales deals that are trusted by leadership or front-line teams. We've implemented a sales technology partially, didn't see results, and then the tool went away in a year, with hours wasted by everyone involved. In fact, we've seen more, and priorities and technology actually take sellers away from sales, with only 28% of time today spent on selling activities.

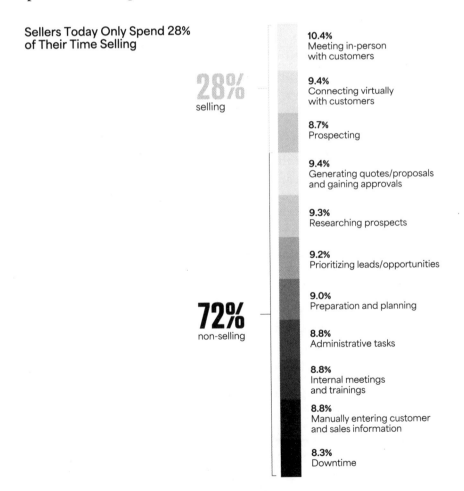

Sellers Today Only Spend 28% of Their Time Selling

28% selling

72% non-selling

10.4%
Meeting in-person with customers

9.4%
Connecting virtually with customers

8.7%
Prospecting

9.4%
Generating quotes/proposals and gaining approvals

9.3%
Researching prospects

9.2%
Prioritizing leads/opportunities

9.0%
Preparation and planning

8.8%
Administrative tasks

8.8%
Internal meetings and trainings

8.8%
Manually entering customer and sales information

8.3%
Downtime

The reasons that salespeople have been averse to technology are understandable. Very few salespeople have actually seen a meaningful impact of modern technology and keep hoping for it to manifest. Less than 40% of CRMs have full-scale adoption within a company. When teams were asked the top reasons for this, with 35% attributing it to technology, 40% believing it's a strategy and deployment issue, and 42% stating that the problem lies with people, particularly the lack of CRM implementation experts or proper training for sales managers.

At the end of the day, technology and AI are here to stay in our sales organization. Now it's time to figure out how to truly integrate our enablement and operations process into one cohesive mindset. We have to get rid of old conventions about technology being for techy operations people and our sales playbooks only being for enablement teams. We need to embrace a new way of thinking that, simply stated, today's technology will transform tomorrow's teams.

Pillar Two of CTAP: How Do We Integrate Sales and Technology with All This History?

With all this history and legacy behaviors, this may be one of the most difficult perceived shifts. For this book, I've analyzed the process that we use to work with companies that are deploying big technology changes or deploying new sales playbooks. I found that the process for proper execution was fairly identical. Whether it was a new technology or new process, it all boiled down to three strategies, covered in the next three sections.

It All Starts with Process First and the Bottleneck in That Process

Every revenue blocker boils down to a gap in the process and not a specific technology need. Even if there is a gap in technology to automate or aggregate something, it all starts by improving a process that removes barriers to sales. Additionally, many organizations focus on solving a small problem here, a medium problem there and assume that all these problems are making a big impact. The reality is that if you solve a million small problems, you still won't see the results you are hoping for, if it's not the one big problem.

This is going to be obvious to any of my supply chain or logistics gurus out there, but in the world of sales, when you ask the average sales leader, they are going to give you multiple priorities and/or bottlenecks that need to be removed. This causes teams to start spinning multiple plates, with workstreams and teams that are working on too many things to actually see an impact. The reality is there can be only one bottleneck by definition. Regardless, many organizations start tackling a variety of problems that never unclog the main issue to revenue growth. Getting that right is key to success.

When you look at these two concepts together, the first step in becoming an integrated sales organization is analyzing your processes, identifying the one bottleneck, and then putting together a comprehensive plan to completely solve that bottleneck, not just partly solve it. You may be shaking your head and saying *of course*. But I further define what I mean by "completely solving" in the next section, and you be the judge.

Identify the Technology Needed to Solve the Process Challenge and Cross-Functional Action Teams

When you understand that all sales challenges are really process problems, the way you'll think about integrating or implementing technology will be different. The Standish Group reported that out of 50,000 new technology projects, 66% end in failure, and the top reason for that failure is lack of buy-in and change management. When we hear about a shiny new tool, we have to always run it through step 1. What is the process issue that it solves? Is that issue the top bottleneck that if solved would be the largest revenue unlock for our sales organization? If the answer is no to the second part, I'm not saying you can only have one process you are working on or that you can't look to implement multiple tools in tandem, but you should really make sure it will have a big impact. In fact when you zoom out and really identify the one bottleneck, it may become clear that this one issue is actually caused by a series of other smaller issues that need to be cleaned up to solve the problem. My caveat here is that it's a slippery slope and it's easy to start adding bottlenecks, which will distract you from driving a complete solution on the biggest issues facing the team.

Assuming you land on the right bottleneck, that's when you think about the right technology to support the process change and develop a comprehensive team to solve the challenge. I've seen teams get one of these right, but the whole thing collapses because they pick the wrong tool, which doesn't solve the real process bottleneck. Or they identify the right process improvement, find the right technology to support that process, and then develop a half-assed plan to deploy it, so the process isn't fixed and the tech goes unused.

The best cross-functional framework I've discovered was developed by Bain Consulting, called RAPID. The reason I like this framework is that it is more encompassing yet simple to execute. You can learn more about this framework at www.bain.com/insights/rapid-decision-making/, but I give you a quick breakdown of how it works for cross-functional teams here:

- R (Recommender): This is the second-to-last person to approve before it goes to the final decision maker (DM). Every project needs one final decision maker, and there can be only one. Depending on the size and scope of the project, this is usually a senior VP or project sponsor if a C-level is the final DM. You can decide how this scales, and there can be two or three recommenders max, but I suggest one final signoff call before presenting.

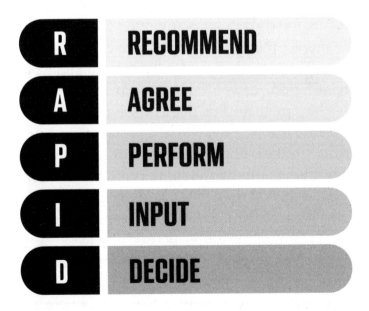

- A (Agree): This is usually the frontline team leaders being affected. This group is usually the key to a successful deployment. In fact, we've come in to save more projects because of messing up the frontline leader involvement than any other miss in a project management plan. They are typically the ones who need to help reinforce the day-to-day, so if you are deploying a process and technology change, they need to have the second-to-last signoff.

- P (Perform): The team that will do the work. This could be a support team, internal business unit teams, or third-party consulting firms such as Skaled. This could consist of frontline managers, reps, enablement, and operations teams, depending on the project type. This team is the engine for the project and responsible for the project management and approval processes as well. This group also helps manage the deployment, which I get into in the last section of this chapter.

- I (Input): We have to get the reps, frontline leaders, and senior stakeholders involved for initial input on the project plan and add their two cents about the end state. It is critical to get feedback from all levels of the organization, or you end up creating something that fits the ops team but doesn't solve anything for the frontline teams. Even worse, a project that senior leadership thinks is important gets minimal input from the frontlines, is run by the support enablement or operations team, and then falls flat on its face on the deployment because the frontline teams aren't bought in. All levels are required here—do not skip this.

- D (Decide): Typically, this is the senior leader whom the project most affects. This is also a critical step. I see projects where the senior leader overly delegates to a support team and the project gets started with deployment and then blows up when the senior leader dips their head in. The perform role should gather substantial input from this role in the input phase and make sure there are regular reviews so the decide person is in the loop. They should basically know what is happening and what will be deployed so there isn't a big surprise at the end.

The quality of the team, its structure, and approval processes will make or break this process. Proper execution means your organization can integrate process and technology and get 90%–100% adoption while solving the bottleneck. The key is nailing both. The more time spent in finding the right tool and team structure to deploy, the fewer headaches you will have down the road.

Implementation Ends at Power Usage, Not Training

Many of these strategies apply to any change-management initiative but are particularly critical for changes involving technology and process changes in a sales organization. The selection process and the team you put together is step 0. The only plan that will solve your bottleneck is one that has deployment go through to power usage. Initial trainings are step 1, but most organizations end up overfocusing on the selection process and try to deploy as fast as possible. After the initial training or deployment, everyone raises their hands, toasts with champagne, and lets out a collective sigh of "Ahh, it's finally done."

Then, three months later, the process has half stuck and the results aren't what you hoped for. These types of process and technology integration projects end up here much more often than not. Why?

My company Skaled is the global leader in sales-specific technology, having completed 500+ sales technology deployments in the sales engagement space alone. We have seen one trend that will really surprise people from our work. Speed to implementation is not indicative of future success. My guess is that for most companies, it's actually a negative correlation. We rush to have a new process or technology live, and it may in fact be "alive," but it's not thriving.

Innovative selling requires us to focus on the final outcome and not just check a box. So to make sure that you see the results from your hard work, consider three very tactical steps:

1. Build the timeline for implementation that ends when you expect to see the outcome from the process/technology change. This will be a big shift, as you won't see results tomorrow, but you will actually see the results that you hope to achieve.
2. Ensure frontline managers are involved in every aspect of the plan and in getting here. In the RAPID framework, I stressed the importance of the frontline leader in the selection and go-live process, but they will be even more important in getting to power usage. Make sure they have what they need to support the team.
3. Align all changes to something that can be tracked, specifically. Many times these initiatives kick off with a plan to solve a problem, but they don't have a specific number tied to the impact of this change.

I've put additional content at resources.innovativesellerbook.com as well. It is impossible to be an innovative seller if you cannot make changes that stick. It's that simple.

Pillar Three of CTAP: Building the Habit of Staying Proficient

The scar tissue from a lack of impact from a sales technology has led many sales leaders to not spend time learning what all these new innovative technologies can do. There are so many new tools popping up, over 2,000 just focused on sales technology, and those tools are evolving. Even when someone thinks they know a tool, it might change dramatically in just six months.

For too long, sales leaders have looked to sales or revenue operations teams to tell them what they need to know and what tools are capable of. Being an innovative seller and sales organization of tomorrow will require sales leaders and salespeople to be proficient at key technologies the same way they are proficient at writing an email or having a structured conversation. This does not mean that sales teams should be out there getting a million technology certifications or that they should spend all their time on tools. It means that tools that are being used need to be fully integrated into their day-to-day workflows *and* they must match the customer journey. Teams that win tomorrow will not see these two things as separate and instead will see them as necessary.

The issue is that sales leaders and reps are pulled in so many different ways—how can they manage? I can't answer this for everyone, but I'll try to give you a tactic that works for me. I call it the 80/15/5 rule.

- 80: I spend 80% of my time focused on activities that will affect my life and business in the next one to three months. We should all be more focused in living in the now vs. the past or future, and the same is true in business. Too much long-term planning can be a detriment to short-term success.

- 15: I spend 15% of my time focused on activities that will affect my life in the next six months. I call this "looking out for future Jake." It's like putting a glass of water by your bed when you've had a long night out. You *must* block out time for things that will affect your life and business in the medium term. I have a weekly standing meeting on my calendar—Thursday morning at 9 a.m.—where I review my six-months goals. Every week I spend one hour going through this and make adjustments to my short-term work to make sure I'll achieve those goals.

- 5: I spend 5% of my time focused on activities that will affect my life in years to come. I have a "bucket list review" meeting on my calendar once a month and have one or two days per quarter blocked out to review our three-year goals for the company. This then informs new process improvements I need to make in the short term. Because I look at the 5%, it can completely change the 80% and 15% buckets.

There are a million books on how to build good habits, and you can learn more at resources.innovativesellerbook.com if you want to go deeper into this pillar. We have to make the time to invest in what will come next and focus on more than this month's or quarter's pipeline; we have to stay proficient in what will come next. My big advice to leaders and sales reps is simple: you must shake the stigma of sales technology and stay up to speed on what is possible.

Summary

When we look at how organizations operate today, it is clear that all sales and revenue organizations must adopt the three pillars of commitment to technology and AI proficiency to be successful. You can no longer have processes that are built on the way that you want to sell when they conflict directly with how customers want to buy. Organizations cannot continue to have separate operations and process improvement groups that are working in silos and not looking at change in a holistic way. Leaders can also not afford to look at technology knowledge as something that can be outsourced to other departments; it is core to being a sales leader and salesperson of the future. Technology is critical for any organization that wants to create an innovative way to drive new customers. They must they adapt their revenue organizations to this new way of thinking.

A majority of this book is dedicated to the third C—the customized sales journey—but with so many organizations struggling to generate the top of the funnel that they need to feed their sales engine, I spend the next two chapters on the second C—current outbound and GTM strategy. Many organizations are using the same plays that were successful 10–15 years ago but today are falling dramatically short. If organizations want to attract more buyers, they must find a new status quo of plays. The interesting part is that the solution here is actually found in the past.

Key Takeaways

- **Join the interconnected world of people, process, and technology:** The modern world is deeply intertwined with people, processes, and technology. Digital advancements and new communication methods are the threads that bind our society. This interconnectedness has led to evolving customer behaviors, highlighting the need for businesses to adapt and innovate.

- **Knowledge is power—leverage technology for sales success:** Harnessing the power of technology, especially using tools such as CRM, can provide invaluable insights to sales professionals. By analyzing data and patterns, salespeople can optimize their strategies. This proactive approach to technology can lead to significant advantages over competitors.

- **Remove the technology stigma:** Despite the evident benefits of technology, there's a reluctance among many sales professionals to fully embrace it. Historical experiences, such as ineffective CRMs or failed tech implementations, have left scars. However, it's crucial to recognize that technology and AI are integral to modern sales organizations. Embracing technology means transforming teams for the future.

- **Integrate sales and technology:** Addressing the challenges of integrating sales and technology requires a thorough understanding of existing bottlenecks and the right technology solutions. The RAPID framework by Bain Consulting offers a structured approach to cross-functional teamwork, ensuring that the right stakeholders are involved at every stage.

- **Implementation—beyond training to power usage:** Successful technology implementation doesn't end with training. It's about ensuring that the technology is powerfully used and integrated into daily workflows.

Speed of implementation isn't the sole indicator of success; the focus should be on achieving desired outcomes and ensuring that the technology is genuinely beneficial.

- **Build the habit of staying proficient:** With the rapid evolution of sales technology, it's essential for sales leaders and professionals to stay updated. The 80/15/5 rule provides a structured approach to time management, ensuring focus on immediate tasks while also preparing for the future. Sales leaders and professionals must actively seek knowledge and stay abreast of technological advancements.

Further Reading

Afshar, Vala, "How High Performing Sales Teams Use Technology to Win in Today's Economy," ZDNet, December 12, 2022, https://www.zdnet.com/article/how-high-performing-sales-teams-use-technology-to-win-in-todays-economy/.

"CHAOS Report 2020," The Standish Group, https://www.standishgroup.com/news/45.

"New Research Reveals Sales Reps Need a Productivity Overhaul—Spend Less than 30% of Their Time Actually Saling," Salesforce, December 8, 2022, https://www.salesforce.com/news/stories/sales-research-2023/.

Scheiner, Michael, "17 CRM Statistics: Growth, Revenue, Adoption Rates & More Facts," CRM.ORG, updated January 12, 2024. https://crm.org/crmland/crm-statistics.

4

The Second C: Current Outbound and GTM Strategy: Pillars 1 and 2

THERE ARE THREE pillars associated with the second C, which centers on changing the paradigm around the current, outdated GTM strategy:

- Sales and Marketing Integration
- Focus on outcomes and not on volume metrics only
- Hyper-customized touchpoints in outbound

For many B2B organizations, the struggle to generate sales isn't closing more deals; it's having enough of the right conversations. The second C and its three pillars focus on how to generate leads in a noisy, complex environment. This chapter is dedicated to the first two pillars, and the next chapter is dedicated to the third pillar because it is one of the biggest fail points for companies: outbound requires a personalized approach.

LinkedIn Is Going to Be Big

It was 2018, and the results were just not what we had seen in any previous year. From the time that I was 1 to the age of 38, I believed the very classic sales mantra. If we can't track it, it doesn't matter. I believed this in my soul, and my consulting firm would preach this to our clients as well. We looked at all outbound and sales activities, and there wasn't a lot of value given to anything that couldn't be tracked directly to results.

Then I started listening to the Gary Vee podcast and others who were preaching the value of social media and brand. What he was saying made sense to me but didn't match my 38 years of life experience, so I was torn. Eventually,

I had an epiphany: "If traditional, outbound tactics weren't working with just a bunch of emails and calls, what could hurt?" In May 2018, I started posting on LinkedIn nearly every day. No ask. No links (cringe) to see how that could inflect results. LinkedIn was just becoming a site for updates and news, but the way Gary was talking about Instagram in the early days reminded me of what I saw LinkedIn quickly becoming.

The results: a bunch of likes, comments, and no real move in new business for our business and clients. We had 0.00 data, other than views, to prove it was working, but something told me this felt right. At about the fourth or fifth month, something happened. We got an inbound lead from a CEO who, and I quote, said to me on the first call, "I'm not sure exactly what it is that you do, but I think we need your help." That deal closed, and that company spent 100k or hundreds of thousands with us over one and a half years.

The light bulb was on and hasn't gone off since. It was clear to me that companies needed to evolve their thinking about traditional go-to-market strategies. Social media wasn't just for marketing teams; it needed to be integrated with sales. By only putting value in what they can track directly to an outcome, companies are shortsighted in what can actually drive impact. It was clear in 2018 that behaviors and strategies were evolving. Today, they are accelerating even faster. Now is the time to take action on the first two pillars if you want to see results in your outbound and GTM strategy, and hopefully our success shows you quickly why pillar 1 is so important.

I have cataloged my innovative selling examples for email, calls, and LinkedIn as well as best practices at resources. inovativeselllingbook.com, so if you need a quick playbook, check it out. My caveat is that if you are looking for a magic bullet, you will struggle to implement the pillars I'm going to lay out in this book. Don't chase a magic template when what you really need is a change in mindset.

Pillar 1: Sales and Marketing Integration

I've been in countless meetings where marketing sat on one side, sales on the other, and both were pointing fingers saying the other was failing. "We are generating the leads, but you guys can't close!" "The leads suck . . . they aren't qualified!" The battles have been waged since the invention of these roles, and they must be fixed for companies to win in today's complex buying world. In *The Five Dysfunctions of a Team*, Patrick Lenconi does an amazing job of illustrating this in an all-too-real scenario, where he walks through a "fictitious leadership offsite," and sure enough, marketing and sales just can't get along. It's almost accepted in many organizations as the "way it is."

Only 23.1% of sales professionals said sales and marketing are strongly aligned (source: HubSpot 2022) and 76% of marketing teams mentioned they're unsure how best to align with sales (source: StrategicAMB 2022). The groups have a long way to aligning, but it is possible with the right strategy and tactical execution plan. The following image is a great example from my own sales leadership career.

ALIGNMENT BENEFITS

What are the biggest benefits of sales and marketing teams being aligned?

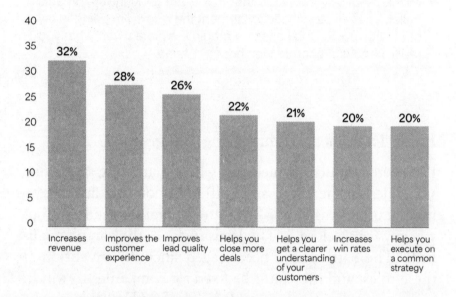

> I use the word *integrated* to describe the first pillar very specifically and not *aligned*, because the two cannot win without each other. Alignment can get out of alignment quickly. When a team is integrated, they are inseparable and work together as one to solve revenue challenges.

I was the Head of Sales for a technology company, NoWait (acquired by Yelp), and we started out in the traditional "alignment" world. Sales was flying solo, sending emails, making calls, and using LinkedIn, but nothing was working. We nearly stopped our focus on enterprise deals because we couldn't get the number of meetings we needed.

Marketing was putting together collateral and organizing trade shows with some success, but the results still weren't there. Out of desperation, we sat down with marketing to discuss what we could do together, and they had a genius idea. What if we recorded custom videos with me and the CEO in the video speaking directly to a specific person, loaded those videos on an iPad, and sent them in a special box to these decision makers? We didn't have much to lose. We invested about $20K in the initial campaign, and then the magic happened. A 75% response rate!

From then on, all of our outbound efforts were done in conjunction with marketing. We became an integrated team because marketing was focused on the goal: book quality meetings. Sales was focused on the outcome as well: let's get meetings even if it's not the conventional way. Fast-forward to today—if teams aren't embracing this strategy, it will be impossible to win. Less than 1.5 years later, we closed nearly $4 million in sale with the play—integration works.

This book isn't going to solve all your marketing challenges, and I don't have silver-bullet advice on how to generate 75% results on every campaign. What I can tell you is that, to win the customer of tomorrow, you need to have integrated teams. You can use the following tactics to start that process:

- **Align incentives and compensation:** If you are a frontline seller, this may not hit home for you, but it's certainly something you should understand. Any time you have groups that are dependent on each other for success, their bonuses and role expectations need to be aligned. Yes, I have seen that just fixing this one area immediately changes the mindset of teams. They become integrated overnight, as they are all focused on the same goal. If you can't affect this directly, the next best thing you can do is set up a "goals and expectations" meeting with your counterparts to better understand their goals, have sales lay out their goals, and then triangulate on a shared set of goals that benefits both. Even if you can't fix compensation, you can create an integrated team.

- **Be responsible for the entire customer lifecycle:** The second necessary step to solving for this pillar is to have both parties 100% responsible for the entire customer lifecycle. Chapter 6 is dedicated to mapping this process. The importance is that marketing can't look at its role as just the top of the funnel support. Marketing needs to be prepared to support each step of the customer journey to give buyers a better experience and take work off the plate of sales organizations when a completely personalized touchpoint isn't required. There are major advancements in technology now, where marketing can help create demos that customers can view asynchronously, create customized landing and renewal pages for individualized experiences, and automate the client testimonial and case study process to close more late-stage deals. Marketing and sales must both be at the table when it comes to shaping the customer experience and journey. Each side brings something different to the table that customers want and expect. More to come in Chapter 6.

After you create an integrated marketing and sales plan, the next step is establishing the lead indicators for sales success that both sides can track and align on. One of the biggest stumbling blocks for teams, even when they are integrated, is picking the wrong leading indicators for outcome production.

Chris McChesney, Sean Covey, and Jim Huling wrote a great book about this, *The 4 Disciplines of Execution* (see Further Reading section at the end of the chapter), where they go deep into this concept. Many companies focus on the outcome metrics, but the game is already being played at that point. Marketing and sales organizations need to focus on the "leads," as *The 4 Disciplines* calls them (defined as measures of activity taken to influence a lag measure), and they have to pick the right ones.

Spoiler Alert: raw activity volume is almost never a predictor of sales success.

Pillar 2: Measuring Outcomes Over Activity

Outbound prospecting is foundationally different than it was three to five years ago. There was a period where we shifted from cold call–heavy teams to email-heavy teams for outbound. It worked for a while, as work email wasn't as clogged with sales emails until the late 2010s. As I mentioned in my story earlier, LinkedIn had also become a great way to cut through, but now it's getting crowded too. These days, billions of emails are sent daily, millions of calls are made, and everyone's LinkedIn inbox is filled with messages about *synergistic opportunities*. The truth is that modern outbound requires more thought and detail than ever before.

It has become clear that in order to differentiate your approach to each individual, you need to execute more complex plays than the typical five emails and cold calls that might have worked in years past. Thanks to technology and process improvements, teams can easily engage with prospects in more complex, customized ways and cut through the noise.

Modern outbound prospecting isn't just about doing more, which, unfortunately, has become commonplace for many sales teams. Succeeding in sales today relies on the *quality* of your touchpoints. As you transition from a quantity-based prospecting strategy to a quality-based prospecting strategy, your company may struggle to make the leap. You may be accustomed to strategies that once worked, such as sending five emails with very little customization and booking a meeting. I wish it were that easy today, trust me, but email and other channels are saturated to the point where bulk outbound just doesn't work.

As part of this trend, I am actively moving many of our clients away from tracking raw activity numbers as a leading indicator to outbound success. Instead, the focus is on the first outcome, which I call "meaningful conversations." This could be a response from a prospect coordinating a meeting or directing you to the right person. You may choose a different definition of "meaningful," but the key is to get the team focused on generating outcomes and not solely on more activity. If Robert can make 15 custom videos a day and hit his number, fantastic. Videos can capture attention quickly and convey a message in a more dynamic way. According to some studies, including a video in an email can increase click-through rates by up to 300%, so why not integrate it? If Brianna is an amazing copywriter, she can focus on 40 highly customized emails and LinkedIn touches a day to get there. The average reply rate for cold emails ranges from 1% to 10%, and the average reply rate for LinkedIn messages is between 5% and 20%, so why not integrate and optimize to find what works best?

This great graphic and report from Mailchimp highlights just how important it is to lean on channels that yield results. You can track LinkedIn inMails in your CRM, but you can't track one-on-one messages between first-degree connections, which I'm guessing most of us would say are even better. So if you are only focused on reps doing more trackable activities, you are missing out on real improvements in results.

	Email	LinkedIn InMail
Bounce rate	0.6%	0%
Unsubscribe	0.3%	0.1%
Open rate	21.6%	57.6%
CTR	2.6%	3.6%

Managing people to outcomes first. Then if they can't get there, look at activity, but I still caution companies from making this the default.

Meaningful conversations are a much better leading number to track for all parties. This also encourages marketing to not focus on webinar attendee numbers or e-book downloads and instead align on conversations generated. When all sides stop tracking raw activity metrics as the "lead" indicator and instead focus on the first outcome, it's like a weight is lifted off the teams and they are all aligned on big-picture outcomes.

Bonus Tip for Pillar 2

The next big trend involves teams breaking out of the NOW NOW NOW mindset. When I talk to individuals and companies, one of the most relevant subjects is how to take a short-, medium-, and long-term approach to prospecting. Every seller must work on a comprehensive pipeline: one that's going to convert in the near term, and one that's going to convert in the medium to long term. After the first two, three, and four months, the medium-term and long-term plans become near-term goals and right-now results. If you dedicate part of your day to planning your book and playing up relationships that may not convert now but will convert in the future (if you're patient), you will enter each month with opportunities. The teams that struggle the most are constantly focused on the short term to the detriment of any type of medium- to long-term process.

Successful outbound and prospecting teams realize that not everybody is ready to buy right now and that many people need to be nurtured. But in four months they'll be ready to have a meeting when budgets come up for review. It won't be just about booking the meeting now; it's about creating relationships that continue to pay off month over month. As you take this approach, you'll engage with people whom you may have connected with five to six months ago. They are now ready to hear what you have to say. Companies have to get rid of the "only things that generate one-to-one results matter" mindset—it's very 2010.

Summary

Outbound today is harder than ever, as the traditional, straightforward tactics are failing. When buying was simpler, the competition was less, we didn't have all these new ways of engaging people, and teams could get away with marketing and sales teams who weren't integrated. When the only way to reach someone was by email or phone, tracking activities had a close correlation to success. Today, people are influenced by so much more, such as LinkedIn posts/comments, that it just doesn't work that directly. As you think about what it takes to have an innovative approach to outbound and GTM strategies, these two pillars are key. As illustrated from my time at NoWait, the teams that integrate and focus on outcomes will have a higher chance of winning, but if the message and strategy isn't personalized, buyers will move on as well.

The next chapter is dedicated to the final pillar of the second C—current outbound and GTM strategies—and is quite possibly the most important for companies wanting to see success today. Outbound, with people in the loop, cannot be successful without personalized content. This may seem controversial as we look to automate more and more, but I'm going to show you why it's an inevitable conclusion.

Key Takeaways

- **Break through the noise:** The number of emails received daily has exponentially increased from 2015 to 2023, making lead generation more challenging. You need to be innovative in your outreach approach, blending traditional and modern techniques for effective engagement.

- **Outbound tactics have evolved:** Early successes with traditional sales mantras focused on directly trackable activities, but the rise of social media, especially platforms such as LinkedIn, has opened new avenues for engagement and lead generation. The value of social media is not just in direct lead generation but in brand building and creating awareness, both of which can lead to indirect benefits.

- **Integrate sales and marketing:** True integration, not just alignment, between sales and marketing is crucial for success. Tactics for integration include aligning incentives/compensation and ensuring both parties are responsible for the entire customer lifecycle.

- **Transition from quantity to quality:** Modern sales success is determined by the quality of touchpoints rather than by sheer volume. The focus needs to shift from raw activity metrics to more qualitative ones, such as meaningful conversations. Focus on building relationships that can yield results in the medium to long term.

- **Avoid using outdated metrics:** Calls and email volumes aren't always the best indicators of success today. Emphasizing outcomes, such as meaningful conversations, over sheer activity numbers aligns teams toward genuine results.

- **Be flexible and open:** Success in today's GTM strategies requires a blend of old and new tactics, with an emphasis on integration, personalization, and a focus on outcomes over sheer volume.

Further Reading

Bump, Pamela, "31 Stats That Prove the Power of Sales and Marketing Alignment," HubSpot, June 8, 2023, https://blog.hubspot.com/sales/stats-that-prove-the-power-of-smarketing-slideshare.

Goel, Ajay, "What's the Average Cold Email Response Rate in 2024?" GMass, December 19, 2023, https://www.gmass.co/blog/average-cold-email-response-rate/.

H. Michael, "How Sales and Marketing Alignment Can Boost Your Revenue Generation: Tips for Early Stage Companies," LinkedIn, April 17, 2023, https://www.linkedin.com/pulse/how-sales-marketing-alignment-can-boost-your-revenue-generation.

Bridge, Oliver, "How Adding Video Will Help You Succeed in Outbound Prospecting," Tapfiliate, March 23, 2023, https://tapfiliate.com/blog/video-prospecting/.

Jezequel, JB, "Cold Email vs. Inmail vs. LinkedIn Message: What Is the Best?" Evaboot, December 5, 2023, https://evaboot.com/blog/email-vs-linkedin-message.

Kearns, Steve, "This Week's Big Deal: Coming Together in 2020," LinkedIn Sales Blog, January 13, 2020, https://www.linkedin.com/business/sales/blog/sales-and-marketing/driving-sales-and-marketing-alignment-in-2020.

Mulkeen, Declan, "Top 10 ABM Challenges [and How to Solve Them]," Strategic ABM, February 15, 2023, https://insights.strategicabm.com/top-10-abm-challenges.

Yang, Suttida, "How Aligning Sales and Marketing Can Generate 209% More Revenue," LinkedIn, https://www.linkedin.com/pulse/how-aligning-sales-marketing-can-generate-209-more-revenue-yang.

5

The Second C: Current Outbound and GTM Strategy: Pillar 3

CHAPTER 4 COVERED THE first two pillars of the second C, which center on changing the paradigm around the current, outdated GTM strategy. This chapter is devoted to the final pillar—outbound must be personalized.

The idea that personalization is critical to generating meetings via outbound and marketing efforts isn't revolutionary. In our consumer lives, we just expect experiences to be customized. When we visit a website or walk into a store, our history is stored and the images, copy, and conversations are all tailored. Amazon shows us similar products based on our preferences, and every streaming service does the same. According to Aberdeen, personalized email messages improve click-through rates by an average of 14% and conversions by 10%, but for anyone who receives cold emails, it feels like 99.9% are just spam.

Today, many people call something personalized by adding: "I see you are the CEO" or "congratulations on some event" or "I see we are in the same industry." I'm not exactly sure when it became acceptable to put in such a poor effort and expect to see results. If this strategy did work at one time, it hasn't for many years. This final pillar of the second C focuses on why personalization at the top of the funnel is required and how to do it at scale.

The Dark History of Sales-Engagement Platforms

Marketing automation tools were created to help build some amount of personalization at scale, but they lacked the ability to customize to a person versus persona and company-based blanket messaging. The only way to do customized emails at the time was one at a time. You had to remember whom you sent the email to and whether the next step was a call or LinkedIn touchpoint because the marketing automation tool only had emails. People would set up task reminders to make calls throughout the process of trying to book a meeting, but there was no easy way to manage all these different types of touchpoints across tools.

Then I saw my first demo of a "sales engagement" platform, such as Outreach and Salesloft, in 2014 and knew it was the answer. Unlike their marketing automation technology counterparts, which were focused on sending a series of emails with custom fields, these tools allowed sales teams to create an infinite amount of steps that could include calls, emails, sending gifts, LinkedIn contacts—you name it. I could create an eight-touch sequence with multiple modes of communication and never have to remember whom to follow up with again or where I was in the follow-up process. You could still have the persona and industry templates that made campaigns successful, but now reps could personalize key messages as well. They hypothetically just gained 20% of their time back from the mundane to now focus on quality, right?

I jumped on these technologies, and my company became the first implementation partner for two of the leaders in this space starting in 2015. Since that point, my company has implemented these tools well over 5+ times, more than any third-party company in the world. This was the magic ticket to amazing personalization at scale.

You would think that by removing all the time needed to remember whom to follow up with, what to do/say, the quality of outreach would skyrocket. These tools even brought in LinkedIn insights. I mean that's like 15% more time available to customize research and insights into each touchpoint. It was a miracle solution.

But instead, we ruined them. Instead of creating integrated, call/email/LinkedIn/video plays, people gravitated toward a slightly better version of a marketing automation platform, with email-only sequences and very little customization. (The same play I ran in 2011.) Because these tools were new, and email wasn't yet overloaded in 2016–18, we were still seeing results with email-only touchpoints. Many sales teams actually stopped doing more personalization because some of the more generic sequences, with custom fields, were working.

By 2018–19, the numbers from email-only sequences, with little personalization, were skyrocketing as sales engagement tools started to reach the masses. Somewhere in 2019–21, many companies had stopped training people on how to do personalized outreach, cold calls, and quality touchpoints as we pushed more of our outbound strategy to email only or email heavy. The problem with that was that email, as a channel, had become overly saturated. Consider these stats:

- In 2018, 124.5 billion emails were sent.
- An estimated 306.4 billion emails were sent and received per day in 2020. Email statistics predict that by 2025, this number will reach 376.4 billion. (See Statista 2021 in the Further Reading section.)

So in just three years, the number of emails sent per day tripled, and they are not done yet. The results were getting worse and worse. By 2022, only 25% of teams reported hitting their outbound targets in a large part due to these strategies.

So you might think that sales leaders recognized that they had a good run with email-heavy sequences and went back to more personalized strategies? The sad answer is no. Today, we still see less than 20% of teams hitting outbound numbers. Even if companies are nailing the first two pillars of the second C—sales and marketing integration and tracking outcomes over activities—they aren't hitting numbers because they aren't embracing personalization at scale.

My hope is that as more people read this book and embrace the philosophies in this chapter, we will move from the dark ages to the golden era with these tools. It is the only way for companies to hit targets, and I have confidence we can do it.

How to Build a Scalable Personalization Engine

The enemy of personalization has been a simple phrase: personalized approaches aren't scalable. These tools that were meant to give us more time to personalize instead turned into automation tools because it was easier to scale. Sending a bunch of emails with a small amount of customization can be automated and is scalable. However, if the results aren't there, we have to look for ways to create scalable processes that aren't completely automated and that actually produce results.

According to research by Salesforce, a whopping 97% of organizations see an improvement in business outcomes due to personalization efforts. Personalization in B2B sales is about understanding individual business concerns of the prospects, their industry, and what their role goes through every day. McKinsey highlights that 71% of consumers expect some form of personalized interaction during the sales process. This makes it essential for sales reps to use customized outreach to connect with relevant prospects. So it's not a matter of *if* you can make it scalable; it's only a matter of *how*.

From my work with thousands of organizations, I've found a common framework for those that do personalization at scale. There are three main elements to creating a scalable process for B2B personalization. They can be repeated over and over again for sales teams, with a mixture of steps that are templated but leave room for customization—mindset, buyer personas, and technology.

Mindset

The first and most important element of personalization at scale is *mindset*. Organizations that are successful today have a simple mindset: they are trying to get a meeting with *one* specific person and will do what it takes to get it. They aren't using a spray-and-pray approach and trying random activities directed to as many people as possible.

They are trying to get a meeting with one person, someone they have identified as potentially the right person who might do business with their company. Buyers are asking for this with their wallets. 77% of customers have selected, recommended, or paid more for products made by a company that provides personalized experiences. However, 74% of buyers feel frustrated when website content is not personalized. You have to embrace this shift and realize that personalization will be required to win deals in the future.

This shift isn't easy for many companies. For the reasons I mentioned in the previous chapter, many companies are stuck focusing on activity metrics as a leading indicator of success. When organizations have an activity-based mindset, they struggle or never fully adopt this mindset. I discussed the need to shift to outcome-based metrics, but there are two other strategies you can implement to help your organization adopt the right mindset:

- Celebrate the meetings you set.
- Add an agenda item to your weekly meetings to highlight meetings set.

A very easy and powerful way to get your teams in the right mindset is to celebrate the meetings you set with key individuals. Make it about the company and person at the company they are trying to set a meeting with. Tell the story of the tenacity or finesse to get a meeting with that one person. It's not highlighting that the salesperson set the meeting only but more so focused on the individual and why they were the right fit. This could be in email, Slack, or other tools, but getting the team to share the strategies they used and the personalization involved will get everyone excited about each meeting set. You can do this with a team of 5 or 500, as it will create excitement around each small win. It will also spark innovation in the team, as people share their strategies and best practices daily, which others can use in real time.

Another way to celebrate or engrain this mindset is to carve out a specific section of each team's weekly meetings to highlight any meetings set with key individuals for a more open conversation. Call out the people that they booked meetings with by name. "Hey, Rachel booked a meeting with Kelly Henderson, who is the VP of marketing at ABC. Rachel had reached out six times to Kelly with various personalized messages about the business and then sent her a personalized video last week that she responded to. Rachel, what was in that video to Kelly?" This type of focus on the individual contact and sharing the strategies will quickly get teams thinking about people and not just activities.

If the mindset of your organization doesn't shift to "our goal is to set a meeting with this one person/company" versus "get out as much coverage to accounts as possible," then personalization at scale will be hard. You need the mindset right first.

Buyer Personas

Next, you have to drill the buyer personas. Even if we have the right mindset and are focused on booking a meeting with the right person, if you don't know who they are, what they do, or what they care about, personalization will be hard. Many of you may already be familiar with the term *buyer persona*, but think of this not just as a job title, which is the mistake most people make, but as a combination of a job title and other factors such as tenure, propensity for risk, and demographics. These combine to give the sales team a clear picture of who a person is and what they care about. You may and will have multiple buyer personas, because there are multiple people involved in the process. It's key then to not only think about the buyer persona of your "buyer" or "end user" but also of the decision makers and other influencers in the process.

Using buyer personas in an email campaign doubled open rates and improved click-through rate five times over (see the Protocol 80 article in the Further Reading section at the end of the chapter). It doesn't just improve meeting conversation rate; it also has a big impact on sales. 71% of companies that exceed revenue and lead goals have documented personas compared to 37% that meet goals and 26% who miss them. We aren't just doing this as an exercise—it is critical for success.

Think of psychographics such as: Is this person someone who wants things that are proven and tested, or is your service a better fit for people who want to be innovative? There are many criteria to consider that need to be included, and it will be important to build this out for each potential buyer or influencer in the process. The following image shows a quick example.

Johnny Smith
CEO (Early Stage)

Age
35-45

Income
$200,000+

Education
Bachelor's, MBA

Employees
5-15

Vertical
SaaS

Influencers
(People who influence their decision making)

- Co-founders
- If they have a leader with a sales background

Key Responsibilities

- Leading the company's overall strategic direction
- Establishing and communicating the vision
- Building and managing teams
- Securing funding
- Overseeing product development
- Driving growth

Goals

- Achieving product-market fit
- Securing funding to drive growth
- Building a strong and talented team
- Establishing the company as a thought leader in the industry

Motivations

- Building a successful company that disrupts the industry
- Creating a lasting impact
- Passionate about innovation, growth, and creating value for customers

Challenges

- Establishing credibility and gaining trust with investors
- Attracting and retaining top talent
- Developing and executing a successful fundraising strategy
- Managing the rapid growth and scaling of the company

Pain Points

- High pressue and stress associated with leading an early-stage company
- Uncertainty of the startup journey
- Constant need to balance long-term strategy with short-term results

Think of nuances to their role versus others in the organization: a CFO may be more likely to care about cost controls and savings, whereas the VP of marketing in the deal may care about growth and new markets. Both of these people work at the same company and deal with similar executive issues but need to be addressed and managed through the process separately.

At resources.innovativesellerbook.com you can find a sample template that will help you when crafting a customer journey so you know whom you are crafting the journey for.

If the team does not know whom they sell to, including the groups typically involved and all the elements of the persona, the team cannot make personalization at scale happen.

One of the best ways to develop the personas is to use Chat-GPT and similar tools. At resources.innovativesellerbook .com you can find prompt templates that allow you to set up ChatGPT to impersonate a person or scenario that you can interact with in real time. It's like having your own CFO, COO, or VP of sales in a box, which you can train to act like your persona. This will help you get better at developing personalized messages for each persona.

Technology

The next element involved in personalization at scale is technology. There are a million tools promising this, but I just highlight the tools that I find most critical. Of course, you need a tool to find people's contact information, but I omit that from here because it doesn't help with personalization. This discussion assumes you already know how to contact them. My favorite tools are:

- LinkedIn Sales Navigator
- Sales Engagement Tool
- ChatGPT and tools like it

LinkedIn Sales Navigator is rapidly expanding as a tool set. Not only can you build lists from your personas to interact with, but you can also build relationship maps that will quickly allow you to reference specific people and ways you can support multiple groups in an organization. Once you save a list of prospects, you can go to the home screen every day, filter by lead shares, and then personally interact with their content. Most people get very little interaction, so when you do this a few times, you will immediately be remembered. This is 5–10 minutes every morning of something that can't be automated, but it is scalable and it will have a dramatic impact on your meeting set rate.

I already talked about the dark side of sales engagement tools, but there is also a golden opportunity to use them correctly for amazing personalization. The way to do this is by using *snippets*. Snippets are smaller sections, usually two to four sentences, that can be added to any template per personas, industries, or other customization. The most powerful application of this that I have seen is when companies create snippets based on subindustries and the size of companies, with persona-based templates. When you take the time to pull relevant customers by exact verticals and group them by size, the results are real. Too often, companies just highlight big companies and non-relevant industries, and the messaging falls flat. With snippets, you can fix that, at scale, and continue to add new snippets to make the companies and scenarios you highlight even more applicable.

The first C—commitment to technology and AI proficiency—calls out AI and tools such as ChatGPT because they are revolutionizing the way people personalize at scale.

ChatGPT can help you get tighter on the value proposition you direct to specific buyers, and it can also help you be specific to the individual and company as well. You can find a more robust prompt library on my website, but here is a good example to get you started:

> Prompt example: "Here are links to ABC's investor relations pages and their press releases as well. I sell a product that helps marketers gain a larger reach with their target audience to grow their website traffic, link here. What is the company talking about that could be directly tied to that? (Please cite the sources.)"

You could also do the same thing with the person's LinkedIn profile and their posts page. Imagine how quickly you could put together a personalized message to an individual about how you can help them *specifically*, including relevant work with similar organizations, and how this all relates to broader company initiatives. All of these plays are scalable, and these technologies make it faster and easier than ever. If you are ready to go deep here, we have actually built a CustomGPT bot for sales organizations that integrates your playbook, Innovative Seller techniques, and serves as each leader's and rep's personal coach in a box. Learn more about it and see our complete tech stack guide at resources.innovativesellerbook.com. The following image shows how to think about your tech stack as you scale.

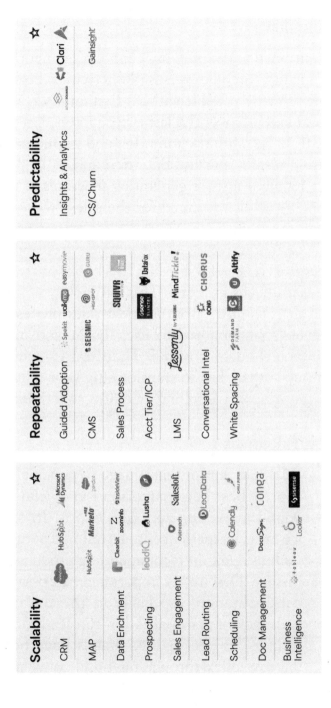

Scalability ☆

CRM	Salesforce, HubSpot, Microsoft Dynamics, Pardot
MAP	HubSpot, Marketo, Pardot
Data Enrichment	Clearbit, ZoomInfo, Lusha, InsideView
Prospecting	LeadIQ, Lusha
Sales Engagement	Outreach, Salesloft
Lead Routing	LeanData, Chili Piper
Scheduling	Calendly
Doc Management	DocuSign, Conga
Business Intelligence	Tableau, Looker, Sisense

Repeatability ☆

Guided Adoption	Spekit, walkme, easymovie
CMS	SEISMIC, HighSpot, GURU
Sales Process	SQUIVR
Acct Tier/ICP	Sisense, Saleintel, Datafox
LMS	Lessonly by SEISMIC, MindTickle
Conversational Intel	GONG, CHORUS
White Spacing	DEMAND FARM, Altify

Predictability ☆

Insights & Analytics	Clari
CS/Churn	Gainsight

Summary

I mentioned in the previous chapter the importance of tracking quality outcomes versus raw activities. Personalization at scale just isn't possible without that mindset. With the strategies I laid out over the last two chapters, I'm confident that any team can shift their mindset and strategies and start generating results quickly. But the concept of personalization isn't required just for generating meetings at the top of the funnel; it is also required for the sales process and the customer experience.

Over the course of the rest of this book, you will learn about these strategies in detail. This will help you build a tactical road map to move from a linear sales process to a process that feels personalized to each buyer and improves faster than you thought possible. The third C—customized sales journey—is the key to transforming your sales organization into an innovative selling machine, so let's jump in.

Key Takeaways

- **B2B sale reps or teams need to personalize their sales approaches:** Personalization is a crucial aspect of outbound marketing and sales efforts. In our daily lives, we expect experiences to be tailored to our preferences, such as Amazon recommending products based on our history. Despite its importance, B2B sales often lack personalization, especially at the top of the funnel. This lack of personalization can lead to missed opportunities, as personalized emails have been shown to improve click-through rates and conversions.

- **Use sales engagement platforms wisely:** Marketing automation tools were initially developed to offer some level of personalization, but they lacked true customization capabilities. Sales engagement platforms such as Outreach and Salesloft emerged as solutions, allowing sales teams to create multi-touch sequences with various modes of communication. However, the misuse of these tools led to overreliance on email-only sequences with minimal personalization, especially as email became an oversaturated channel.

- **Create a scalable personalization engine:** The misconception that personalization isn't scalable has hindered its adoption. However, research shows that personalization significantly improves business outcomes. To achieve personalization at scale, companies need to adopt the right mindset, understand their buyer personas, and leverage the right technology.

- **Shift your mindset to personalization:** Successful organizations prioritize personalization by focusing on individual prospects rather than adopting a broad approach. Celebrating successful meetings and sharing personalization strategies can help instill this mindset within teams.

- **Understand your buyer personas:** Buyer personas provide insights into potential customers' preferences, needs, and concerns. They go beyond job titles and consider factors such as tenure, risk propensity, and demographics. Properly crafted buyer personas can significantly improve sales outcomes, making them essential for effective personalization.

- **Leverage technology for personalization:** Tools such as LinkedIn Sales Navigator, Sales Engagement platforms, and *Generative AI* tools such as ChatGPT can enhance personalization efforts. These technologies allow sales teams to gather insights, create personalized outreach strategies, and engage with prospects in a more tailored manner.

Further Reading

"12 Buyer Persona Statistics That Prove Their ROI," Inbound Marketing Blog, Protocol 80, https://www.proto col80.com/blog/buyer-persona-statistics.

Artug, Esat, "44 E-commerce Personalization Statistics to Inform Your 2023 Strategy," NineTailed, December 31, 2023. https://ninetailed.io/blog/ecommerce-personalization-statistics/.

Ceci, Laura, "Number of E-mail Users Worldwide from 2017 to 2026," Statista, August 22, 2023, https://www.statista .com/statistics/255080/number-of-e-mail-users-worldwide/.

"Create Personalised Emails Your Customers Actually 'Get,' Want & Read," Digital Marketing Institute, March 30, 2015, https://digitalmarketinginstitute.com/blog/create-personalised-emails-customers-actually-get-want-read.

Dubzinski, Jane, "Benefits of Personalization in B2B Prospecting," DemandScience, May 17, 2023, https://demandscience .com/resources/blog/importance-of-b2b-personalization/.

6

The Third C: Customized Sales Experience

RECALL THE 4Cs of the innovative selling framework:

- Commitment to technology and AI proficiency;
- Current go-to-market (GTM) strategy (adjustment of);
- Customized sales experience/journey; and
- Consistent performance optimization.

The first five chapters of this book were critical to understand, and I hope you paused between each chapter to take one small action. If you didn't, I encourage you to go back to Chapter 2 and start documenting just one change you can make to how your team views technology and is running its outbound and GTM strategy today. Now it's time to talk about the heart of the matter, building an innovative selling process.

The core concept of this and the following chapters is that the customer journey must be mapped and optimized for ideal experiences at each step. Historically, B2B sales strategies were often rigid, following a one-size-fits-all approach. However, the digital revolution has ushered in a new era where adaptability is key. Over 90% of B2B sales organizations now recognize the efficacy of an omnichannel strategy, marking a significant departure from traditional methods. This shift toward a more dynamic sales process is not just a trend but a necessity, driven by the diverse needs and preferences of modern buyers. Companies that cling to outdated, static sales methods risk being left behind in a market that demands agility and personalization.

It is interesting to watch how many organizations start building their sales process by implementing a one-size-fits-all sales methodology and then retrofitting it to their buyers.

The process seems a little backward and always has to me, which is why we start by defining the customer journey in the first pillar and then dive into finding the right processes for the sales journey to interact with buyers at each step.

When you take this mindset into your sales process, you ensure that your sales organization knows where a customer is in their buying journey so they are prepared to have a productive conversation at each step. The ultimate win-win.

To build customized sales experiences, you have to start by mapping the customer journey. This process cannot be skipped. This is the process for how you take various buyer personas within your ideal customer base through the process based on their preferred ways to interact. These customer journeys—yes, plural—serve as a way for everyone in the organization to understand the best way to engage and work with customers throughout the buying process.

When you take the time up front to invest in these three activities, before finalizing the sales process, you ensure that your process is set up to optimize your customers' experience. Now let's dive into personas and ideal customer profiles and how you do (and don't) build these critical components of your sales process.

Pillar One: Mapping Your Customer Journey and Experience

The year was 2021. It was late December, and I had a few loose ends to wrap up before the end of the year. One of those loose ends was prepaying for a few of our key technologies, as we had a bit of cash surplus at the end of the year. I contacted our largest software expense provider to pay for our licenses up front. We had two new reps that year, so we pinged support on who the contact was. I won't mention the company specifically but . . . about 75% of companies I know use this tool. About two or three days later someone got back to us. I was traveling and asked the rep where I could find a link to pay with a credit card. It was about $40K–$50K annually, and I wanted to pay that day if possible. His response was utter confusion and the classic "Before we get there, can we set up a call to discuss your needs?" email. He pushed again for a meeting, and I very directly said that I would be happy to meet with him in the new year to discuss, but I wanted to do the renewal now. He pushed for a call again; I said no and politely asked for the link to pay with credit card. Obviously, a software giant like this company had this ability in 2021, right?

No, they did not. He sent me a PDF into which we had to enter our credit card details and send it back. I was shocked at how far behind they were in understanding their customer journey. Like many organizations I talk to, the reason the experience was so bad is that he had been trained on one *linear* process. He only knew that process because the process was not set up for today's modern buyers who are more informed and technology savvy than ever before.

Currently, 65% of the workforce consists of Millennials and Gen-Zers, who are digital-first buyers. They prefer to conduct most of their buying journey anonymously, avoiding direct interactions with sales representatives. This behavior is changing across the board with buyers across generations now preferring a self-serve experience. They want to find information on their own, try products before buying, and validate marketing and sales claims with trusted customer proof. The use of sales representatives in the research process has declined, with only one out of four buyers consulting them first in 2022, an almost 20% drop from 2021. You need to make sure you build a process that matches what your buyers want and not how you are used to selling.

To fix this mindset, we have to break away from building a process that begins with "What's our methodology or sales playbook?" when the question we should be asking is, "What is our ideal customer journey?" This is where it all starts. If your company hasn't mapped your various customer journey options or you haven't tried it personally, you are in the right place. There is no time like the present to step back and think through the customer experience, even if you have done some work here or have been in sales for decades. The modern customer journey looks very different than it did in 2010, so the rest of this chapter is dedicated to changing the way you think about the sales process by aligning your focus on a customer-first and methodology/playbook second. Let's jump in.

Consider the Customer

What you really need to determine is the optimal experience for your customers. Of course you likely have multiple customer journeys, so as you go through this exercise, think about ideas like:

- How would you handle a persona that has already vetted your competitors and is looking to make a decision quickly?

- How would you handle a customer who set up a meeting via a cold email and doesn't know the space?
- How can you build a process that meets the customer where they are in the journey and helps them navigate the process as quickly as they need to, with as little friction as possible?

Today you also have to consider different modalities you are using to interact, as opposed to your typical "hop on a call." A McKinsey study showed that in just five years the amount of interaction points buyers have with a brand has doubled (see the Further Reading section for more details). This may seem a bit overwhelming at first, but process really isn't that difficult to start.

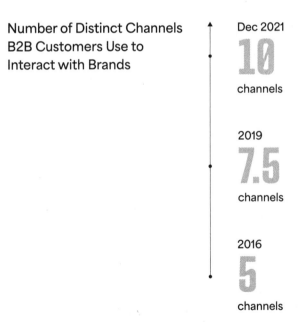

Number of Distinct Channels
B2B Customers Use to
Interact with Brands

Dec 2021
10
channels

2019
7.5
channels

2016
5
channels

I usually find it's best to get a small group from marketing, sales, and account management together for a three to four-hour exercise, but you can do this solo as well. The first step is more of a qualitative approach and an approach you have to take if you don't have hundreds or thousands of customer data points to analyze, which help you understand the customer journey of your best customers and customers that stick with you for the long run.

Most B2B sales have a similar rhythm, which can be elongated or shortened based on the complexity of the sales. That process includes the following stages (you may use different names):

- Discovery
- Initial evaluation
- Formal evaluation or pilot if applicable
- Onboarding
- Initial adoption
- Power usage and growth
- Renewal

I include the post-sale steps in the book because, as we think about our customer journey map, this is what matters to the buyer. A sales methodology that is only focused on the initial sales process is going to miss every time.

The first pillar starts by taking a step back and starting with a few very basic questions. I've included a template for you to use to help to guide you through it on the website resources .innovativesellerbook.com as well, but it starts by thinking through the process of your customers and detaching yourself from your product and the excitement about what you do.

CUSTOMER JOURNEY MAP

Stages	Stage 1	Stage 2	Stage 3	Stage 4	Stage 5	Stage 6
Actions	▮▮▮	▮▮▮	▮▮▮	▮▮▮	▮▮▮	▮▮▮
Thoughts						
Feelings: Positive / Neutral / Negative	●	●	●	●	●	●
Pain points						
Opportunities						

91

Whether you are an executive or a frontline rep, this exercise is extremely valuable; it's worth doing every six months or so.

Start by acting like one of your buyers, and ask yourself these questions:

- What would you need to see to want to engage with your company? Would you want to see a piece of content, social proof, or what would move you to engage?
- What would you want to see next? Once you have engaged with your company, what would be ideal to see next? What would help you before talking to someone once you have engaged?
- When would you want to talk to a person or have a person help guide you in the initial stages of the process? What about the next step? And so on.

You can keep going through these three questions for each stage of the process until you get to ideal interaction points for each step based on a specific buyer's intent and interaction type preferred.

> Before you access the template, I suggest you read this chapter and the next to get your creative juices flowing. It can be a great chapter for teams to read together before the exercise. It can help them to think through what an ideal customer journey looks like.

The main output you are looking for isn't just one straight-line customer journey, but typically three to four journeys based on the persona purchasing or initial entry point. It should be a process map that shows the best case for the customer and focuses on their journey and not just how sales "qualifies" or shows up in the process. Start and finish this process with the customer in mind. Make sure you think about the nuances of how customers initially find you and interact with your brand, because the journey starts there. Think about how you can create a fast-track process for very educated and vetted buyers and a separate track for someone coming in blind. (I go into detail on this process in the next chapter.) The more time you spend mapping your various customer journeys today, the more time you save down the road guessing at your sales process.

Example Customer Journey Exercise

Let's jump into an example here to get started. I walk through the first few steps, and you can run from here. This might mean a customer journey map for a marketing technology that sells to the digital marketing group and helps track conversion rates across various marketing channels.

Example: one persona COMPANY A sells to is the VP of paid advertising in the finance industry.

- They typically find out about us from:
  o Cold outbound
  o Industry trade shows
  o Some inbound but they haven't really responded to paid ads from our team.
- What happens on the cold outbound path:
  o Usually this means they may not be in the active evaluation stages.
  o They may not have heard of us.

- o They might not be happy with their current partner.
- o *Typical next step is an educational call to get them excited and to understand their priorities. We need to be prepared for a more in-depth call if they are more educated.*
- ▪ Alternative: They come in from an inbound path:
  - o They are usually actively evaluating.
  - o This could be a smaller company, so we may need to send them a few questions up front.
  - o They might want a prerecorded demo as well because they have some knowledge of us.
  - o *Typical next step is that they want a demo and pricing sooner in the process, assuming they answer questions up front, so we need to make sure they can get that on the first call.*

What will start to become clear almost immediately as you work this process is how different buyers are as they start the process, which means the linear process just doesn't work for everyone. What also starts to become apparent quickly is that you have to try to understand where your potential customers are in the buying process. How much do they know about your product, and what is their level of intent? You need triggers that signal whether you should move faster or slower, depending on these variables.

Summary

Mapping the customer journey will be an immediate wake-up call for any sales team member or leader. The mindset shift from "What does this person probably want?" to "Here is our process we use," can be both empowering and a little scary, as you think about mapping your process to multiple paths. The sales team will also need to account for the second pillar, developing a process that can triage high-intent prospects through the process. You have to make sure your new innovative process has components to move high-intent buyers through the sales process differently than those with low intent. The sales experience must meet each person where they are in the process and guide them along appropriately.

Key Takeaways

- **Build an innovative selling process:** Over 90% of B2B sales organizations now use an omnichannel strategy, emphasizing the shift from traditional methods. Companies that don't adapt risk being left behind in a rapidly evolving market.
- **The customer journey should be your primary focus:** It's essential to define the customer journey first and then determine the best processes for the sales organization to engage with buyers. By understanding where a customer is in their buying journey, your sales teams can have more productive conversations.
- **Mapping your customer journey is crucial:** The process of mapping the customer journey involves understanding the various buyer personas and their preferred ways of interaction. This mapping serves as a guide for everyone in the organization to engage with customers effectively.
- **The modern buyer's behavior has changed, and so should you:** Modern buyers, especially Millennials and Gen-Zers, prefer a self-serve experience and want

to conduct most of their buying journey anonymously. The role of vendor sales representatives has diminished, with fewer buyers consulting them. Sales processes need to adapt to these changing behaviors and preferences.

- **Consider your customers' perspective:** Different customers have different journeys, and your company should be prepared to cater to each one. Your sales process should focus on the customer's journey and not just on how sales qualify or show up.

Further Reading

Donchack, Lisa, Julia McClatchy, and Jennifer Stanley, "The Future of B2B Sales Is Hybrid," McKinsey & Company, April 27, 2022, https://www.mckinsey.com/capabilities/growth-marketing-and-sales/our-insights/the-future-of-b2b-sales-is-hybrid.

Drenik, Gary, "What Significant Shifts in B2B Buyer Behavior Means for 2023," *Forbes*, December 13, 2022, https://www.forbes.com/sites/garydrenik/2022/12/13/what-significant-shifts-in-b2b-buyer-behavior-means-for-2023/?sh=70bb0a641c43.

7

Engineering Your Sales Process for Speed

In the last chapter, I mapped the various paths that a buyer could take based on the way they bought historically. This should include who is involved at which step, actions they take, and how the groups work together. If you did not complete that exercise, that's okay, but after you finish this chapter, it is a must. Without a clear picture of your customer journey and experience, it will be impossible to build an innovative sales process. The second pillar in creating a customized sales experience is engineering your sales process for two things: speed and picking the right path for a buyer based on their intent level. That's the focus of this chapter.

Fixing the B2B Buying Process

As mentioned in Chapter 6, many sales organizations are not optimized for speed today. Forcing people to get on a call, holding back price, and many other traditional sales tactics create buyer friction. According to a Gartner survey, 77% of B2B buyers say their latest purchase was very or somewhat complex or difficult. This suggests that there is a significant amount of friction in the B2B buying process (source: Gartner 2023 B2B Buying Report).

Some of the common friction points that B2B buyers, not sellers, experience include:

- Difficulty finding relevant information
- Long and complex sales cycles
- Lack of transparency
- Poor sales experience

According to a Salesforce survey, 57% of buyers have abandoned a purchase due to a poor sales experience. This suggests that a significant number of buyers are willing to go elsewhere if they don't have a positive experience with the seller (source: Salesforce State of Sales Report 2023). The really entertaining part of these studies is that many times I hear similar statements from sales teams. "Their internal approval process is complex," "I'm not sure who does what," "They aren't getting back to me"—these are all statements I've heard hundreds of times from B2B sales organizations as well.

These old-fashioned, manual steps don't align with how buyers want to consume information today. They want links to videos. They want to read an article on their phones with a glass of wine. They want to scroll through feeds when they wake up. They want to find something they like, click purchase, and have it show up tomorrow. B2B buying just hasn't caught up, but this pillar can help you modernize your customer journey. Of course, your customers most likely will still want to talk to a helpful person at some point in the process, but where that happens and why can vary greatly.

Pillar Two: Getting High-Intent People through the Process Faster

I've heard horror stories from B2B buyers wanting to buy a product and being forced to sit through several initial meetings, where there was zero value for them. The "qualification" call is solely for the benefit of the selling company, but what happens when the buyer is three steps ahead and comes in close to the finish line?

Take a step back and think about what this process looks like from the outside. You have a potential customer, someone interested in a solution. They reached out to the sales organization to learn more and then were handed off to someone for an initial conversation who asked them a bunch of level-one questions. When the seller described the product, it wasn't tailored to this customer's needs. This experience aligns with a Salesforce survey that found that 82% of buyers say that it is important for sellers to understand their needs and challenges, marking it as the top expectation of buyers from sellers in 2023 (source: Salesforce Sales Report 2023).

It is critical that you take the time to go deeper into the customer journey exercise and understand the customer's path not only based on the persona but also based on how they found you and what should happen next. In line with this, according to a study by Conductor Academy, consumers are 131% more likely to buy from a brand immediately after they consume early-stage educational content. This suggests that educating buyers early in their journey is an effective way to increase sales (source: Conductor Academy 2022).

The study also found that the impact of educational content on buyer behavior is long-lasting. A week after reading educational content, consumers were still 48% more likely to buy from the brand that educated them. When given a lineup of four brands to purchase from, 83.6% of consumers chose the brand that provided them with educational content. So if it helps to get buyers educated up front, then we should look to build an experience that helps these educated buyers move through the process faster.

We talked about buyer personas in the previous chapter, and the focus of this chapter is to ensure that you build customized paths for each persona based on their level of interest and intent. Imagine having multiple paths of the customer journey based on intent. These aren't big leaps, just slight variations of your customer journey, which will allow you to help customers get to the next stage faster.

There are really just a few ways the people find you and therefore just a handful of sales processes that each company needs to account for. I'll introduce an easy concept that will help you understand what real intent looks like, called vetted, educated, and cold.

Vetted Customers

Vetted customers must have performed at least five of these actions in order to be considered vetted. Note: They do not have to be a decision maker.

- Have met with a competitor or reviewed their offerings online
- Have used this product at a prior company
- Have researched your offering via a peer or online resource
- Have an understanding of pricing
- Have a clear business outcome they are looking to achieve
- Have a clear timeline
- Have already defined the evaluation process

Educated Customers

Educated customers must have completed at least the three actions below to be considered:

- Have researched your offering via a peer or online resource
- Have a clear business outcome they are looking to achieve
- Have a clear timeline

Cold Customers

Cold customers, by definition, have completed fewer than three of the criteria in the educated customer description. The goal before interacting with a potential "cold" customer is to educate them before you meet with them so they can self-guide and you can meet them at the educated stage. This should be done digitally as much as possible.

Build Individual Journeys

With these definitions in mind—which you can tweak slightly for your sale or business—think about where customers are when they find you. You need journeys for each persona that account for the following:

- Cold prospects you reached out to first;
- Warm prospects that requested a demo;
- Hot prospects that may want to self-guide or maybe even want to self-service and talk to someone later; and

- Prospects who start moving quickly and get to "hot" in the early stages after a first call.

I find that this typically takes an additional one to two hours per persona to think through how to fast-track each of these four paths. I assure you that this exercise is worth the additional time, as it will allow you to move people from cold to educated quickly and get the vetted leads to close much faster. Many organizations skip these steps, implement a sales methodology, and work backward.

The Individualized Customer Journey

This section walks through two *amazing* customer journeys from beginning to end, so you can see why having different journeys is so critical. Same job title, same industry, same years of experience, and everything else on paper looks the same, but the way we treat these two buyers couldn't be more different.

Example 1: Mike the Digital Marketer (Buyer/Influencer)

Mike the digital marketer (buyer/influencer) needs a marketing solution to better track attribution across his team. He is a member of a "digital marketing strategy" Slack channel and pings the group asking their opinion on tools in a certain price point tier. He gets four recommendations and goes directly to the websites of those companies. He then does a little more digging and identifies his top two. He reaches out directly to book a demo.

One company, which takes the "sales methodology first" approach, has a sales development rep reach out to Mike.

This person isn't qualified to give insight and focuses on qualifying Mike. Mike is annoyed because he already did his research and now is delayed a week, until he can get someone else on the phone who can actually help him. He is frustrated and can't understand why he can't get information faster.

He then goes to the second company, which is using an optimized customer journey. They fast-track Mike because they understand his intent level *before* the first call. They do this by asking Mike a few questions up front and getting the right person on the first call. Mike's first call is with a sales rep and sales engineer, who are prepared to discuss details and pricing options. They then move to proposal the next week and are able to set up all the relevant demos and pilot calls in two weeks on a potential $200K sale, which is twice as fast as a typical enterprise sale. This company recognizes that Mike is a vetted buyer and moves him through the process in a way that he wants to move. The first company had their second call with Mike with a sales rep who basically asked the same questions as the SDR and then booked a meeting a week out to loop in others. It was obvious they weren't interested in how ready he was, so he goes silent on them and starts the procurement process with the second company immediately. The second company won because they met Mike where he was and helped him to make a decision faster.

Example 2: Lisa the Digital Marketing Director (Buyer/Influencer)

Lisa is also a digital marketing director (buyer/influencer). She gets a series of cold emails and a thoughtful message on LinkedIn from a sales rep. She is annoyed that she can't track attribution of marketing channels, a product the sales rep sells, but currently has other priorities. She agrees to take the meeting, as she is interested in seeing what is out there.

She takes the meeting, and the rep asks some very specific questions that get her thinking about how the data issue is affecting her team. The salesperson then gives a high-level overview of how they typically support digital marketing leaders, which piques Lisa's interest. She hasn't identified a budget for a solution or exactly how she will deploy it, but she does see some potential. On the next call, the company's goal is how to help Lisa move to the "educated" bucket, where she can start to identify how she might pull this together if her team loves it. She brings it up to her leader, who says to explore it if there is a return on investment. Her team hops on the call and immediately sees the benefit. They talk in their next meeting about how the potential impact would benefit them. Lisa then sets up a call with the rep to discuss pricing rollout options to get a better sense for where it might land.

This is a customer journey in which someone comes in cold. In this case, you need to do more nurturing, provide proof cases, and build trust to get the potential customer to the vetted stage and further along in the process. Again, it's all about meeting your buyer where they are.

The pricing is laid out, and the salesperson suggests a proof of concept to show Lisa's leader the ROI from the product. They agree to a 60-day proof of concept, and the sales team knocks it out of the park. Lisa converts to a $200K customer and is thrilled at the impact this has on her team.

Breaking Down the Two Scenarios

Note that both of these potential customers had the same job title, company size, and function. However, they required different approaches, based on their knowledge and experience with the product or market. To ensure you give the right experience to each customer, you need to know where they are in that journey. Mapping your customer journey to account for various personas and levels of intent ensures each customer has the right experience.

The bottom line? According to a McKinsey study, companies that personalize their sales experience based on the customer's journey see an average increase in sales of 10%–15%. Additionally, the study found that companies with personalized sales experiences have a 15%–20% higher customer satisfaction rate (see the McKinsey article in the Further Reading section).

Another study by Salesforce found that buyers who have a personalized sales experience are 140% more likely to make a purchase. In today's innovative era, companies cannot afford to have a process that isn't built for speed and the right touchpoint at the right time (see the *Forbes* article in the Further Reading section).

Bonus Section: Product Lead Growth (PLG)

PLG has become a major go-to-market strategy over the last few years, as more companies look to have their product be "sticky" enough so that sales teams only

---

(continued)

need to get involved at critical points in the customer journey or even not at all.

I love this mindset and can see it work specifically for products that have low monthly per-user costs and don't require substantial collaboration with IT or across departments. Consider Slack and Canva as the poster children for this movement. They built a product that could be shared in small groups in the same department, or used by individuals, and once those groups started to expose it to other departments, they were intrigued and started using it. These products spread across groups and the PLG company sales team start to get involved to do a rollup or enterprise deal at some point in the process. Meeting buyers where they are in their journey and understanding how they want to buy is critical to any modern sales organization. If it works for you to do free trials at the end user level, then by all means—make it happen.

When you build a PLG sales organization, you have to break the way you think about building traditional sales organizations.

You can't build outbound early. You can't build "hop on a call" into the pitch. You can't "over-qualify prospects." The product should be leading most of this process. The product, not the seller, determines who is the best fit. There are many software companies using AI to analyze user behavior and come up with the exact right time for sales to engage. This is the future of many companies in how they inform sales when to engage, PLG or not.

Let's walk through a typical PLG customer journey of a larger company. (In Chapter 9, I talk more about the proof of concept process, which you will see comes into play even in companies that use the PLG go-to-market plan.)

The Canva tool makes design simple and easy for everyone. It is used by marketing, design, sales, and many other departments when they need to make engaging presentations or design without a professional designer.

They have seen explosive growth, and their last valuation was in the nine figures. How did they do it? They gave away a basic free version and made the pay version very affordable for anyone to put on a company credit card. In 2019, they decided they needed an enterprise sales motion and hired Skaled Consulting, my company, to help them build out the outbound sequences to engage with companies that started to see high usage to start rollup deals. We've worked with Figma and Mural in a similar capacity over the last few years as well.

In a PLG motion, the goal is to have the product become sticky via its own utility and marketing, and then once it reaches a critical number of users, the

(*continued*)

company has sales reach out to key pockets to see about a roll-up in that group. This is what Canva did. Once you do that, you might reach out to senior department leaders to give them the option to roll up further. Then once you get multiple departments using at scale, you might reach out to procurement to do a master agreement across the organization.

As you can see, once a company with a product-led growth (PLG) organization gets a certain amount of traction, the customer journey starts to look a lot like a more traditional land-and-expand model.

When you are building your customer journey, consider whether you should have a PLG path as well. It could become a major part of the journey if product, not sales, is driving the movement between steps.

Summary

When you take the time to map the customer journey before you build your sales stages, you ensure that your customer experience is world-class. When you define the ideal customer profiles and match the right journey to each persona with intent levels, you give your customers the best sales experience based on their desired journey. With this mindset, you can be flexible enough to adapt to the

modern buyer and ensure that more people become customers faster.

The following image is a great summary of where we are
headed. Digital interactions and the ability of customers to
find information on their own is becoming the cornerstone
of the modern buyer. Push yourself and your company to
look for ways to meet buyers where they are, as much
as possible.

WHAT BUYERS WANT IN 2023

 75% of buyers prefer virtual iteractions with salespeople and a more self-service approach.

 40% of buyers named "having to contact sales for a demo or free trial" among the three things vendors do to make them less likely to buy.

 81% of buyers want to find pricing information on their own.

 55% of buyers say reviews are one of the most important factors when evaluating solution providers.

After you've identified the personas and the right companies, and mapped your various customer journeys, it's now
time to map to your sales stages to build a customized sales
journey.

Key Takeaways

- **Map the customer journey:** Without understanding the customer journey, it's impossible to innovate the sales process. Every interaction, from the first touchpoint to closing the sale, should be carefully analyzed and optimized. To develop targeted and more effective sales strategies, be sure to recognize different customer personas and their respective paths.
- **Speed is crucial:** Modern consumers seek quick, frictionless experiences when purchasing. Traditional sales tactics, such as holding back pricing details or mandating calls, can deter modern buyers. Make sure your sales process reflects contemporary buying behaviors, prioritizing speed and efficiency.
- **Fast-track your high-intent customers:** Tailor the sales experience based on a customer's level of interest and intent. Vetted leads, who already have significant knowledge and interest, should be pushed through the process swiftly.
- **Know the difference between vetted, educated, and cold leads:** Vetted leads exhibit numerous signs of intent, such as having met with competitors or researched the product extensively. Educated leads have a foundational understanding of your offering and a clear objective. Cold leads need nurturing and education to transition them from unaware to potentially educated or even vetted customers.
- **Adapt your sales tactics based on customer entry points:** Not all customers start their journey at the same point; adjust your tactics based on the customer's initial interaction. For instance, a warm prospect who requests a demo should not have the same journey as a cold lead who knows nothing about the product.

■ **Tailored sales experiences lead to better outcomes:** Mapping specific customer journeys to different intent levels and personas ensures that each potential customer receives an experience tailored to their needs. Aligning your sales process to match the customer's desired journey can significantly improve conversion rates and customer satisfaction.

Further Reading

"B2B Buying: How Top CSOs and CMOs Optimize the Journey," Gartner, 2023, https://www.gartner.com/en/sales/insights/b2b-buying-journey.

"Educational Content Makes Consumers 131% More Likely to Buy," Conductor, April 6, 2022. https://www.conductor.com/academy/winning-customers-educational-content/.

Lindecrantz, Erik, Madeleine Tjon Pian Gi, and Sefano Zerbi, "Personalizing the Customer Experience: Driving Differentiation in Retail," McKinsey & Company, April 28, 2020. https://www.mckinsey.com/industries/retail/our-insights/personalizing-the-customer-experience-driving-differentiation-in-retail.

Morgan, Blake, "50 Stats That Prove the Value of Customer Experience," *Forbes*, September 24, 2019, https://www.forbes.com/sites/blakemorgan/2019/09/24/50-stats-that-prove-the-value-of-customer-experience/?sh=151abaab4ef2.

"State of Sales Report," Salesforce, 2022, https://www.salesforce.com/resources/research-reports/state-of-sales/.

8

Mapping Your Sales Experience—the Early Stages

RECALL THAT THE third C is the customized sales journey and that involves mapping the customer journey for an ideal experience, getting high-intent people (vetted customers) through the process faster and creating a custom mapped sales experience.

This chapter and the next two cover the process of creating a custom mapped sales experience. In fact, over the course of the next three chapters, I am going to get very tactical on how you can handle each step of the sales process and all of the nuances that happen throughout the customer journey. This chapter breaks down the foundations of a world-class sales process. Some people might call it the Innovative Seller Methodology, but at the end of the day a methodology means very little if it doesn't incorporate all the elements of being an Innovative Seller. Think about this chapter and the next two as the railroad tracks that show you all the stops and key milestones of this customer-centric sales process.

Good Sales Follows a Process, but Not a Rigid One

Many people believe that sales is a dark art that just happens because people are charismatic or can build relationships. Some think because people are social or like to talk that they can be good at sales, but the reality is that sales is much more of a process than people realize. Without a process, you can't provide an ideal sales experience because there will be wild variability from salesperson to salesperson.

I learned the importance of process specifically when I was 26, after starting my first job in tech sales. I started my sales career in professional sports, working for teams in Major League Baseball and the National Hockey League. After two and a half years, I was ready for a change and found an amazing opportunity with a technology company that had just opened up an office in Phoenix. I was six weeks into the job and was one of the last people to make a sale in my training class. This was baffling to me, as I had been a top performer in all of my previous sales roles and couldn't understand why I wasn't closing deals. The director of sales pulled me into his office after listening to one of my calls— this conversation changed my life. We started the conversation with me voicing my bewilderment as to why I hadn't closed a deal. I had no answers.

He asked me how it was going, and I laid out for him that I was struggling. He asked me whether I was following the script and process, which made me laugh. "Ha . . . scripts are for amateurs, and I like to make sure I have a conversation." That made my director laugh, and he looked at me with a straight face and said something I'll never forget. "Jake, do you think we are dumb? Do you think that we train a thousand sellers on a process that doesn't work?" He smiled and waited for me to respond. I thought about it for a few seconds and said, "Well, I guess not." He then proceeded to ask me to try it, to drink the Kool-Aid and go all in on the process. Since I hadn't made a sale, I said why not, and I went all in.

The result from executing the well-designed, tactical process that was customer centric? I sold $60,000 in new business the next month. Yes, I sounded a bit robotic as I worked on the messaging, and yes, it was uncomfortable following such a rigid process, but when I heard how people responded, I was hooked. My eyes were wide open, and I realized that sales was much more of a process and system than I had ever imagined.

Over these next three chapters, I break down all the *stages* that go into a world-class sales process. This will include the *steps* that are critical at each stage of the sales process, as well as other core nuances of the process that sellers need to know. I cannot emphasize this enough, do *not* implement these stages and steps without doing the customer journey first. This book is not intended to replace MEDDICC or insert other methodology that is one-size-fits-all. These stages and steps should be *different* based on persona and intent, so keep that in mind as you map your customized sales journey.

Here is how I define these stages and steps:

- *Stages of the sale:* These are the big leaps in the customer journey. Think about those moments where a customer jumps from one part of the sale to the next.
- *Steps in each stage:* These are the actions that happen in each stage of the sale. Each stage of your customer experience has action items that indicate whether it's time to skip ahead or move forward to the next stage. You might call these "exit criteria," but unlike with the linear 2015 sales process, the buyer is excited about the process vs. forced through it.

So to keep it simple, think of stages as the big leaps in the process and steps as what actions have to be executed in each stage to move to the next stage. Frontline sellers may initially look at this chapter and think that this is for their bosses or execs, but I can promise you that the best reps spend time breaking down their process and making it actionable.

What Makes a Sales Process Successful Today

Many sales organizations are still set up to qualify people when many customers have already done their research. So they are qualifying buyers when these buyers are already signaling intent. I talked about this in detail in the last chapter, but I want to reiterate the issue here, because it will not survive the next five years.

Many companies have created a conveyor-belt sales process that hands the customer from person to person with minimal care for what happened and information gained in the prior step. To build a guide for your customers and sales process, you have to focus first on aligning each role in your sales organization to the optimal experience for the customer. It should either help customers get to the next step faster or move them out of the process due to poor fit from both sides.

Here are the stages:

- Discovery
- Initial evaluation

- Formal evaluation (or pilot if applicable)
- Onboarding
- Initial adoption
- Power usage and growth
- Renewal

This chapter focuses on the steps in the sales experience that you need to map to the early part of the customer journey. I argue these are some of the most important steps, because they determine how to approach the customer early in the process. It has always been one of the more vital parts of the sales process, but in today's "speed first" world, speed to information and speed to meet a customer where they are in the process are critical. Let's consider these early stages of the customer journey in more detail.

The Discovery Stage

Sales teams must determine how educated this potential customer is. They also need to determine which groups will need to be involved in this sale, and they need to consider whether they can provide the customer with asynchronous education **before** the first meeting. Interestingly, 19% of buyers want to talk to a sales rep when first learning about a product. You need to move away from the old-school mindset of "qualification" and view your role as "consultation," with a goal of understanding many factors, including intent and education.

A study by the *Harvard Business Review* found that companies with a well-defined discovery process are more likely to close deals and achieve their sales goals. The study also found that these companies have a shorter sales cycle and higher customer satisfaction rates (see the Further Reading section). The discovery process sets the stage for the relationship, so it is important that it is tailored to the potential new customer.

The controversial take I have here is that sometimes discovery should happen not on a call but on the buyer's timeline.

How Much Knowledge Do Your Potential Customers Have? In your customer journey map, you should map how customers came to this point. Perhaps marketing or an outbound effort has led someone to book a discovery call to learn more. The person may have no background or may be fully prepared to discuss details. You need to be prepared for either scenario and assume that they are somewhere on the spectrum between fully educated and cold.

When you are mapping this part of the sales experience to your customer experience, make sure to think through this. It's the most common miss I see in the sales experience, as most teams are trained to get on the phone and qualify before ever showing the product. As you can see from this image, there are many factors that contribute to a buyer's decision process, which is why the discovery stage is so critical. If you don't have the right questions, sellers will consistently miss key pieces.

B2B PURCHASE DECISION INFLUENCERS

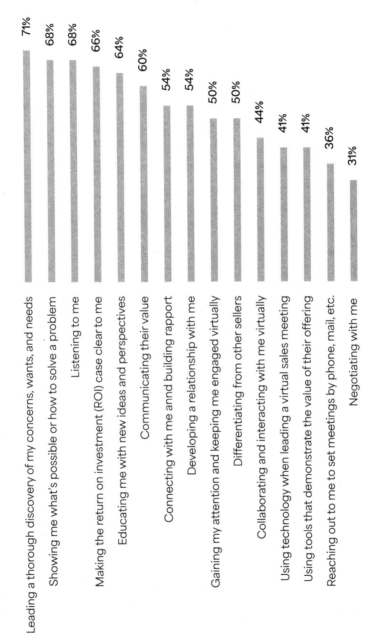

Leading a thorough discovery of my concerns, wants, and needs — 71%
Showing me what's possible or how to solve a problem — 68%
Listening to me — 68%
Making the return on investment (ROI) case clear to me — 66%
Educating me with new ideas and perspectives — 64%
Communicating their value — 60%
Connecting with me annd building rapport — 54%
Developing a relationship with me — 54%
Gaining my attention and keeping me engaged virtually — 50%
Differentiating from other sellers — 50%
Collaborating and interacting with me virtually — 44%
Using technology when leading a virtual sales meeting — 41%
Using tools that demonstrate the value of their offering — 41%
Reaching out to me to set meetings by phone, mail, etc. — 36%
Negotiating with me — 31%

Either way, prepare for the person you are meeting by reviewing their background on LinkedIn or use ChatGPT and review their company online. The key is that buyers expected a person in the loop only if they are prepared and understand their business.

To move on to future stages in the process, you need to think about which actions are critical for the customer to take at this step. You'll want your sales experience to capture the following:

- Whom am I talking to, and how do they fit into the org? This shouldn't be an interrogation, just an understanding of what this person does matched to a typical persona. This is key, as not every VP of marketing does the same thing.
- What is their level of education of the problem, and how much vetting have they done to date?
- What are their key challenges?
- Be ready to address how your company typically solves their problems, if they have them, at a high level. You have to be ready, on the first discovery call, to have a business conversation if the prospect is already educated or vetted.
- Be ready to lay out the next steps in the process clearly and concisely based on their intent level.
- Get the person excited for the process.

Here is the difference between the above and what many organizations do today. Today you need to handle these steps before a first call, when possible, with marketing content, videos, or other content, and don't push to make everyone "hop on a call" to do a discovery.

From my years of experience, there are a few questions to ask as you decide how you want your sales team to show up at this stage:

- *Decision making path:* According to Gartner, the average B2B buying decision involves six to ten people, each of whom is armed with more than four pieces of information they've independently gathered as part of their own decision-making process (see the link for Spotio in the Further Reading section).
- *Intent level:* As discussed in the previous chapter, you must know how educated they are about the various solutions and what step they are at in the buying process.

What's super-important to know here is that you *do not* need to get all of this in your first conversation if it doesn't fit the customized sales journey. Instead, you have to think about how your best-fit customers find you and move through your specific process.

For example, if your best customers always have a budget set aside for purchases like yours in advance, it makes sense to talk about budget during the first call. If your best customers usually come inbound with someone looking to gather information, then establishing the decision-making process may be critical up front. Each customer journey is different, so in this first stage of the process, you need to map what is ideal for your buyer. If you don't have enough data, that's fine as well ok. Make basic assumptions, and test them over time to optimize.

What Are the Customers' Needs?   Decide on the level of completion for your best-fit customers that needs to happen in this first conversation (or what you capture in advance) and on the criteria to measure it.

If customers do not meet the criteria that you developed, it's important to have a talk track or digital experience in place to give them alternatives. Your job is to help customers make the best decision possible, whether that is with your organization or not.

Additionally, when you have a customer that is not ready or does not feel they have a need or issue now, that's more than fine. In these cases, it is important to leave the customer with a few potential scenarios, which, when encountered, means that you should reengage the conversation. These almost always are cold prospects. I want to give you a few tactical ideas about how to move cold prospects to educated in the near future.

Here is a good talk track to set the stage for cold prospects in the discovery that could become educated in a short time because they now are more aware of the problem:

"It seems like things are going well and that business is thriving right now. If XYZ happens over the next two to three months or ABC, then it makes sense that we should reconnect then to discuss a potential plan forward."

I've seen this work extremely well. When you check back in a few months they many times say, "Glad you reached out; we actually have had ABC happen and it might make sense to connect." Doing this leaves the door open to potentially new conversations in the immediate future and also makes the customer keenly aware of the problem you solve. Now they will be looking for these issues and will better understand how you can help.

Who Else Makes Purchasing Decisions? After you have conducted some type of discovery, the buyer will typically need to loop in others. If your first point of contact was with someone higher up the chain, they will want to loop in the team that will be using the product. If you start with one person in a key group, most likely they will want to loop in a broader team before wanting to introduce you up the chain. Again, this isn't universal. You need to map your experience to the cold, educated, and vetted buyer.

Many times salespeople push this process and try to force meetings that don't fit with how customers actually vet and select providers. I'm all for pushing to get people involved, but the more you show that you understand the process of how people really make decisions, the more the customer will view you as the expert.

After the discovery process, I move into the key steps of the sales process that move the customer from light consideration to closing the sale. These steps serve as the foundation for your sales process, after mapping the customer journey, so make sure to take notes about what configuration is the best guided journey for your prospects.

The following sections cover a few other nuances and sales process best practices before you dive in so that you have a full understanding of what goes into a world-class customer experience.

Over the rest of the sales portion of the customer's journey, there are usually multiple stages that involve looping in more people from both sides, evaluating various internal and competitive options, negotiating, and then setting the customer up for success with onboarding. I dive into each one of these stages here and over the next two chapters and cover ways to optimize the customer experience at each step. Because of this complexity, even with smaller deals or transactional sales, execution at this stage is key. Any small miss can lead to deals not closing.

Discovery is the most important part of most customized sales journeys, and is the ability to understand where someone is in their intent level so you can move them quickly through the process. If you do not take the time to think about what the discovery process should look for buyers that come in with various levels of intent, you will just recreate the old-school, one-size-fits-all discovery process that treats people the same—nobody wants that. Now let's jump into what happens after you understand what the buyer needs and where they are in the process as they move into the initial valuation.

An absolutely critical variable here is guess what. Buyers might reach out to you already in this phase! So that's why the process to understand where someone is in the process early is so critical. We might need the vetted buyers to start at this stage. We probably need to design a process that starts at this next stage: initial evaluation.

The Initial Evaluation Stage

The initial evaluation stage is where you and the customer agree that there might be potential alignment. You both agree to loop in other people from both sides, share additional information relevant to the deal, and move forward with learning more. Today, I've seen buyers show up on the first call with multiple buyers. So make sure you are ready if they are.

The move from this stage to formal evaluation is where companies struggle, either because the sales process becomes too complex for their internal team to handle or the customer realizes the complexity of the solution and chooses to do nothing.

Drive Momentum Forward to Help the Buyer   This is also where the customer begins to rule out various competitors and options because a company is not a good fit or they don't trust that a company can actually help them. The latter is the reason that many deals go dark and why many organizations struggle at this step. There is misalignment between what the sales organization is saying and what the customer believes may be possible. Keep in mind that the buyer might have already narrowed down a few potential partners at this time, so what will you do? Keep moving people through the process slowly, and hold back information or make sure you are ready to get the right information to the buyer as fast as possible.

Remember, customers don't care about signed contracts like salespeople; they care about outcomes and solved problems. An innovative seller and organization makes sure they understand that a new potential customer cares about the go live and success with the product early on in the process. Keep in mind a buyer who is educated or vetted has already talked to the people internally that need to say yes, so if you don't start talking about the go-live process early, another innovative sales organization will. This is why you have to talk about the onboarding and the go-live process in the sales process early. When it's not discussed or people don't trust what's being said, they will choose either to do nothing or go with a competitor.

Consider All the Stakeholders, Not Just the Decision Makers   This stage is made even more complicated with the introduction of new influencers and decision input personnel, where this stage will be their first interaction with what you do and who you are. Most sales organizations and methodologies struggle to understand this nuance, and therefore the process can become very sales driven instead of customer centric. This is because the sales organization knows how to execute a cookie-cutter approach and not how to customize the process based on what they have learned throughout the sales conversations.

In a true customer-centric approach, you must focus on the experience of all the stakeholders—their various intent levels and unique concerns—to ensure that before you enter the next stage, which is the formal evaluation, each key stakeholder understands how your company can (or can't) align to their goals. A startling statistic reveals that only 13% of customers believe a salesperson can understand their needs (see the article by Brian Williams in the Further Reading section). This underscores the importance of truly understanding and addressing the needs of stakeholders. Remember, in a more complex sale, you might have different people in the same company who are at different levels of education. So in your customer journey map, make sure you account for that.

If you sell a more transactional sale where there are only one or two people involved in the process, the logic is the same. Every sales process needs to consider what complexities might exist based on how their customer likes to find information, move through the process, loop in others, and ultimately use the product. Everyone has at least one other person that they talk to before making a decision, and the goal is to get that person involved as quickly as possible to ensure they have the right information so you can align what you do with their goals and needs.

The key to a real customer-centric process is appreciating that there are steps and other people involved. You don't have to force your process on people, but instead you should accept how customers want to buy and meet them where they are.

Whether your sale takes one or two calls to close or two years to close, the elements are the same. They just happen at different speeds.

Use Separate Solutioning: Now Is the Time to Stop Reading and Start Really Taking Notes   The biggest nuance you need to account for when designing your sales experience at the initial evaluation stage is the concept of *separate solutioning*. With separate solutioning, it doesn't matter whether the other people involved are three to four divisions in a large company or one or two people in small business—the key to understand in the initial evaluation stage is that it is the salesperson's job to meet with each individual stakeholder and their unique challenges and needs so that in the end you can address those in the formal evaluation stage. A seller today cannot simply rely on one person to relay information across the org and schedule everything. An innovative seller must understand that if you want to move a deal forward, they have to be the person who helps each individual person in the buying process move from cold to vetted. Without this mindset and plans in our customer journey map, we will consistently build a process that doesn't match the preferences of each stakeholder.

It is important to think about the digital touchpoints in your sales process at this point as well. Many organizations lack content or digital strategies to keep various buying groups engaged. Here is one of the most important stats in this book: only 17% of the buying process happens between the buyer and seller, so what are we doing during the other 83%? This means having a digital strategy here is critical.

Distribution of Buying Groups' Time by Key Buying Activities

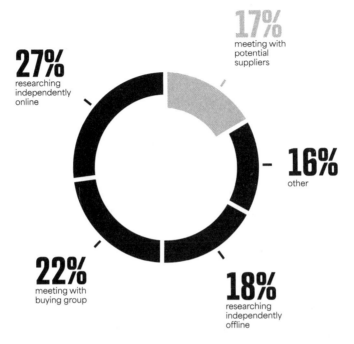

17% meeting with potential suppliers

27% researching independently online

16% other

22% meeting with buying group

18% researching independently offline

When you combine a digital experience and add a salesperson to the process, you'll see much better engagement across the buying group. You are looking for a customer to go on a mutually agreed upon journey after they loop in other people. That is when you have a viable sale—not before. I'll continue to iterate that buyers will come to you who are already at the point of viable sale when they first reach out. So how do you plan to map your customized sales journey for buyers who have looped in others, shown their team videos/demos, and then show up on a "Contact Us" form but you didn't have record of them in your CRM? The answer is how you handle the discovery stage. Keep all of this in mind when you do the customer journey map.

Summary

Before you move to designing your sales experience for closing and onboarding, make sure to pause and go through the process in this chapter with your team. This book is meant to help sales organizations think differently and, more importantly, to take those ideas and put them into action. Whether you are a frontline rep or a VP, you can make small changes to your process today. I implore you to take this seriously and make a change today. The first two phases of the customer journey, covered in this chapter, are critical. They determine when and how you should move to later stages, to ensure that your sales organization and you personally are ready to get people moving if they come to you educated or vetted.

Key Takeaways

- **Understand your sales process:** Sales involves a systematic approach that demands a strategic mindset. A methodical, customer-focused process can significantly elevate sales outcomes. View it as a guided journey.
- **The customer journey should be your primary focus:** It's essential to define the customer journey first and then determine the best processes for the sales organization to engage with buyers. By understanding where a customer is in their buying journey, your sales teams can have more productive conversations.
- **Approach the discovery phase with an open mind and thorough preparation:** This phase is vital for gauging the customer's needs, their level of knowledge, and intent. Preparation at this stage can encompass reviewing customer profiles on platforms

such as LinkedIn and understanding their company's operations.

- **Segment your sales process into stages and steps:** The stages represent significant milestones in the customer's journey, and the steps are actions in each stage. They should be clearly defined in order to guide customers seamlessly through their journey.

- **Address the needs of all stakeholders during the initial evaluation stage:** This stage is pivotal for discerning potential alignment between the seller and the buyer. Any discrepancies or misunderstandings at this juncture can jeopardize potential deals. You need to be prepared to move people to this stage in sales interaction point one when you have vetted buyers.

- **Use separate solutioning:** Salespeople need to interact with all stakeholders individually, addressing their unique requirements and challenges. Active guidance from the salesperson throughout the process is essential, rather than relying solely on a single "champion." You also need to have separate customized sales journeys for different people in the process.

- **Understand the role of the seller:** Sellers are the linchpins in propelling the sales process and liaising with all parties involved. They must be proactive in steering customers through the journey, ensuring alignment at every step. Sellers should be agile, especially when interacting with customers who are well informed or exhibit strong buying intent.

- **Embrace change:** Try novel strategies and translate innovative ideas into action. By being adaptable and responsive, your sales teams can cater more effectively to educated and vetted customers.

Further Reading

Chetan, Kumar, "Is Sales Art or Science?" LinkedIn, May 17, 2020, https://www.linkedin.com/pulse/sales-art-science-kumar-chetan.

Dopson, Elisem, "Understanding the B2B Buying Proces: The Key Factors and Stages That Affect B2B Decisions." Shopify, December 5, 2022, https://www.shopify.com/enterprise/b2b-buying-process.

"What B2B Buyers Say Sellers Can Do to Influence Their Purchase Decisions." MarketingCharts, April 16, 2021, https://www.marketingcharts.com/industries/business-to-business-116798.

Williams, Brian, "21 Mind-Blowing Sales Stats," The Brevet Group, 2023, https://blog.thebrevetgroup.com/21-mind-blowing-sales-stats.

Williams, Rachel, "7 Sales Statistics Salespeople Might Not Know (but Should)," Calendly, February 15, 2022, https://calendly.com/blog/7-statistics-salespeople-might-not-know-but-should.

Zoltners, Andris A., Prabhakant Sinha, Sally E. Lorimeer, and Chris Morgan, "Now Is the Time to Shake Up Your Sales Processes," Harvard Business Review, October 23, 2022, https://hbr.org/2020/10/now-is-the-time-to-shake-up-your-sales-processes.

9

Mapping Your Sales Experience— During the Late Stages

As YOU CONTINUE to the later stages of the customer journey you may be tempted to think that understanding intent and readiness to buy is less important than in the early stages. At this phase, the buyer may be closer to a decision, but many deals stall out or are lost because salespeople don't take care of easing the buyer's fear of purchase or address the plan to get started quickly. We talked about this in the last chapter because we have to be prepared at all steps in the process to talk through the go live and implementation from the first conversation if buyers are ready.

The biggest fear of B2B buyers is making the wrong decision. This is according to a study by Gartner, which found that 63% of buyers said this was their biggest concern (see the Gartner article in the Further Reading section). The study also found that other common fears of B2B buyers include:

- Choosing a product that doesn't meet their needs (58%)
- Overpaying for a product (53%)
- Getting locked into a long-term contract with a vendor they're not happy with (49%)
- Experiencing poor customer service (47%)

As other stakeholders enter the picture, they may have their own agendas and timelines that change from the earlier stages. Even at this stage you need to look for cues from various stakeholders that may be further behind or ahead so you can meet them where they are. You need to think about how your sales journey will ease these concerns at key moments and help to make it easier overall to buy.

This chapter breaks down the later stages of closing the deal and the onboarding process, which is the logical extension for the customer when you are designing a sales experience. As I'll repeat over and over—the customer cares about using the product and not signing the contract. The contract is a milestone in the process, but it's not the end goal for the buyer. This chapter also breaks down how to run an effective proof of concept process if you have a sale that requires a buyer to test the product.

First, let's dive into the formal evaluation. Typically this means that both sides have invested time and resources into the potential partnership and are interested in seeing what a potential path forward looks like. When you are considering the customer experience, it will be critical not to focus on the typical sales process mindset behaviors and instead think about how to better enable buyers to close.

The Formal Evaluation Stage

You are now heading into the final sales stages of the customer's journey. At this point, if you execute correctly, you have a chance at gaining a new customer. Don't assume that your company is the only one the potential customer is considering at this stage.

During this stage, discussing the onboarding, initial usage, and power usage phases of the sales process are *just* as critical as price negotiations. Why? Most people fail to see that a major reason they are losing deals isn't because of the competition; it's because the company makes no decision or moves forward with a partner who is further along in the process.

In today's digital world, most buyers expect quick responses from businesses they want to work with.

As you progress through this stage, it is critical to spend time talking about onboarding and addressing customer concerns.

For companies to be successful in the formal evaluation process, they need to make sure their sales experience conveys the following:

- A clear business case that allows them to show value and impact in real terms
- A clear plan for implementation
- Their role in helping during each step of the process

As mentioned, even if you have a very transactional sale or a simple product to implement, these concerns are all still very real.

Self-Guiding Is Key

An important part of mapping your sales experience is to understand whether you should add a pilot or proof of concept to your journey. Some products need to be experienced first, and you might have a PLG model that depends on it. Don't be afraid to build in a self-service part of your process as well. You read in previous chapters that many buyers want to self-guide. Your journey should account for people who want to self-guide, talk to someone, and then possibly self-guide again. The numbers of such buyers are growing quickly, even ones who are willing to make big purchases without a seller at the final step.

Check out this image from McKinsey that shows people interested in making big purchases end-to-end digitally. Many organizations may be shocked by these numbers, but I suspect they will continue to grow, so make sure you have multiple pieces of the process, even the final stages, whereby buyers can self-service.

% of Survey Respondents Who Said They Would Purchase Through End-to-End Digital Service And Remote Human Interactions for a New Product Or Service

OVER $1M
amount **15%** are willing to spend

$500K TO $1M
amount **12%** are willing to spend

$50K TO $500K
amount **32%** are willing to spend

In this next section, I lay out how to create a win-win customer experience if you do need a proof of concept in your process.

Consider a Proof of Concept

Let's start with why you would or wouldn't want to utilize a proof of concept/pilot in your sales process. I would like to see everyone move to the term *proof of concept* because the whole goal in trying something or using it for free should be to prove the concept—or prove it's not a fit. No trials and wait and see. No pilots to test it out. Two groups moving toward a common goal that, if successful, will lead to a partnership. If it's not successful, it will prove that buyers and sellers are not in alignment for the time being. An article from gtmnow.com mentions that their conversion rate of POC-to-business wins was 60%, especially in the context of a high-growth startup with a lot of competition (see the Mangum article in the Further Reading section).

You should use a proof of concept if your product, when demonstrated successfully, has a high conversion rate. You should not use a proof of concept, at least not consistently, if your product is difficult to implement or requires extensive time to see benefits (unless you can make a 6–12-month proof of concept potentially).

When you have a proof of concept or trial, there are several elements that you have to make sure you control in order to ensure success:

- The right KPIs for success. Hopefully this has been laid out in your customer success plan, but if not, you need to establish the POCs criteria. You should suggest metrics to the customer that you are confident you can hit.

- Reestablish a budget for phases past the proof of concept. There is no point in doing it if they can't move forward.
- Confirm any additional "decision paths" that are needed to move to the next phase of full partnership.

You should avoid a proof of concept in cases in which:

- There isn't much room to grow past the initial sale—the first sales is kind of it; or
- The product is not annual subscription based. If they can cancel, then just use the first few weeks/months to prove value.

Once you have decided which path is ideal for your customer to evaluate the product, you can decide which path is right for you. Again, just like all the steps in your process, you need to make sure your sales experience accounts for different buyers with different needs. Remember, this is about the customer journey and your team building a customized sales journey to match each buyer where they are in the process. This is going to come as a surprise to many people, but at times, a proof of concept can actually be a required step in the sales journey. The story I mentioned in chapter 4 about NoWait, the Current GTM Strategy chapter mapped to this exactly. After our marketing and sales teams were aligned, and we then accepted that a POC was a part of the process, we moved that customer from $0 to $4 million in 10 months because of the play I laid out above.

I see a lot of companies not understanding the principle that more meetings can actually move deals faster. More meetings to align stakeholders instead of hoping they figure it out on their own can make a huge difference in success or failure. Instead of waiting for two people to sync internally, you can be the person who helps the collaboration happen. Things will move much faster this way. More meetings = faster deals.

The Closing and Onboarding Stage

The final phase of the traditional sales cycle is the closing process. One potential sale might go through all these stages in a matter of weeks, and others might take months; it all depends on how educated your customer is and their level of intent. Feel free to adapt the previous examples to your business. Here are the most common factors I see leading to a deal:

- Every key group has a path to onboarding.
- You have been introduced to procurement or the final person signing the contract.
- You have confirmed where you are in the process compared to competitive solutions.
- You have solidified a signing date and onboarding date.

A majority (27%) of B2B buyers say the biggest factor in their purchase decision is competitive pricing. Other significant factors include having a broad range of flexible, high-quality products (cited by 25% of respondents), offering fast resolution of issues (24%), demonstrating value for the money (22%), providing speedy and efficient service response (22%), and allowing buyers to contact the vendor at a time that suits them (21%) (see the Kristensen article in the Further Reading section).

TOP FACTORS OF IMPORTANCE FOR BUYERS

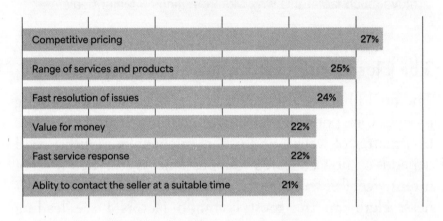

Competitive pricing	27%
Range of services and products	25%
Fast resolution of issues	24%
Value for money	22%
Fast service response	22%
Ability to contact the seller at a suitable time	21%

If you have these factors in the deal, you should feel confident that a deal is close, so make sure your sales experience shifts to meet clients' expectations so the potential customer understands the next steps in going live.

When many people think of sales, they immediately think of the close. The person signing on the line. In reality, modern sales is really a series of events where signing the contract is a step in the process that is typically more important to the selling organization than to the customer. In your customers' mind they think of things in terms of vetting the solution, ensuring the budget is ready to go, getting alignment with key groups internally, putting together a plan for go live, finalizing the contract, and then the real work starts getting the product utilized. Signing the contract is not the end game for your buyers—it's the beginning!

> My big tip here is that if you find yourself losing deals at this stage, I can guarantee that your sales team isn't explaining the onboarding process in enough detail to make people feel comfortable going live. Any time you have deals that have fallen off in your pipeline this late, investigate the stage before. Can't find any issues there? Then go back to another stage. You may be missing critical questions that are killing you in the close or later stages. The answers are there if you are willing to go deep.

At this stage in the process, you are trying to drive toward the onboarding stage and initial user adoption, so the main goal is to get the implementation plan in motion, *presales*. Put the customer in the process, and help them clearly understand what's going to happen next so they can rest at ease that everything will be handled with their purchase.

In order to move to the onboarding phase, you need to focus on having two actions verified. It's important to start this process *before* the contract is signed:

- Scheduling plan for subsequent trainings or onboardings with various stakeholders
- Schedule for key reviews of the business value and return

Every organization should focus on getting all of these steps secured before they hand off to the onboarding process or, if you have a team, to the onboarding team.

If you work in an environment where you also handle onboarding and management, it's important to acknowledge this is a new phase in the relationship and treat it as such. They just signed a contract—they are excited—now you need to make everything sticky. Having a specific onboarding process is critical to that.

When the customer signs, the real work begins. The client has signed the contract and has the relevant people ready from their side to go. What happens over the next weeks/months, depending on your product, will make or break your potential renewal in months or a year from now. It's critical to spend a significant amount of time in your customized sales journey map on this phase.

When clients "fail to launch," you find yourself having to go back stages in the process to reestablish a plan and realign stakeholders on the benefits and the reason it is so important to go live now.

It's perfectly okay to schedule the kickoff and set up meetings before contract signing. In big deals, you should be bringing in your team during the formal evaluation stage. The move from onboarding to initial usage is probably *the* most critical step in the sales experience when it comes to likelihood to renew.

> Let me repeat this—the most critical step in the sales process and a happy customer experience is the move from onboarding to initial usage.

These are key elements of success I've seen for a good onboarding process:

- Don't anchor or compensate on speed; this incentivizes horrible behavior to move packs of customers through who are not ready.
- Do establish metrics for use in each key department that, whenever possible, are based on previous client behavior and usage:
  - Logins/usage;
  - Appropriate amount of usage during a target period; and
  - Percent of people using.

A big mistake I see companies make is trying to automate or "help desk" too many people and then have major churn problems in the future. Try to make the process as customer centric as possible from the get-go. Use the right amount of hand-holding to get as many people as possible to the initial usage, and then look to back out people and make the process more automated or technology enabled.

I tell every client the same thing. Just because someone leaves the initial onboarding stage once doesn't mean that some clients won't come back to this stage if they are struggling. If they keep coming back, there is a good chance they were not a best-fit customer in the first place. Sales should be looped in to help if the problem persists. The usage metrics to move to "initial usage" will vary, so pick what is most applicable to your business.

The only additional criterion to exiting the onboarding stage is that all future meetings should be scheduled in advance. Don't get sloppy and make assumptions. Get all your ducks in a row so your team can execute properly.

Summary

So much of customer churn is simply due to teams not having a set process for working with their clients after the sale or setting the right expectation during the sales process. Fix this issue, and you will have a stress-free transition. Now you move to the part of the sales experience that will help you create customers for life: initial and power usage. When an organization views its sales experience all the way through the process, with the end goal being to create power users, it changes behaviors earlier in the experience. Companies such as Hubspot even built in compensation rewards for sellers whose clients renew.

Before you go on to the next chapter, I encourage you to pause and make sure you have truly mapped and thought through your late-stage customer experience. This will ensure that your sales team has what they need to give the customers what they need at the end of the deal. Then think about ways you can surprise and delight throughout the onboarding process.

There is a great book called *Never Lose a Customer Again* by Joey Coleman (2018) that can help you to ideate on new, interesting ways to get customers excited through this phase. The book specifically calls out various media such as video, in person, email, and others to consider how to make the handoff smooth and entertaining. Remember, at these stages, your customer just made a big purchase—they may be nervous—so think about how your late-stage customer experience can have a dramatic effect on your ability to create customers for life.

Key Takeaways

- **Understand the late stages of sales:** These later stages involve understanding the buyer's intent and their readiness to purchase. Steps that can prevent deals from stalling include addressing a buyer's apprehensions and ensuring a swift initiation plan. As more stakeholders get involved, their varying agendas and timelines can shift the dynamics, necessitating a tailored approach to each.
- **Enable buyers to finalize their decisions:** The formal evaluation signifies mutual investment from both parties, aiming to explore a potential partnership. Onboarding and post-sale steps are as vital as the sale itself, in order to ensure that the buyer's journey is smooth.
- **Consider a proof of concept (POC):** A POC is essential when a product, once demonstrated, has a high conversion rate. POCs should have clear KPIs for success, a reestablished budget for the post-POC phase, and a confirmation of any additional decision paths. (POCs might not be suitable for products with limited growth potential or those not based on annual subscriptions.)

- **Treat closing as the beginning:** The act of closing a sale is not the end but a significant step in the customer's journey. Focus on the onboarding process and ensuring that the buyer is comfortable with the next steps.
- **Prioritize the customer's needs during onboarding:** The onboarding phase is crucial for setting the tone for the customer's experience. Establish metrics for success during onboarding, focusing on logins, usage, and the percentage of active users.

Further Reading

"B2B Buying: How Top CSOs and CMOs Optimize the Journey," Gartner, 2023, https://www.gartner.com/en/sales/insights/b2b-buying-journey.

Coleman, Joey, *Never Lose a Customer Again*, 2018, London, UK: Portfolio, https://joeycoleman.com/books/never-lose-a-customer-again/.

Kristensen, Emil, "11 Surprising B2B Sales Statistics You Need to Know in 2023," May 24, 2022, https://www.drip.com/blog/b2b-sales-statistics.

Mangum, Freddy Jose, "Sales Proof of Concept (POC): 5 Ways to Drive More Revenue," September 16, 2021, https://gtmnow.com/sales-proof-of-concept/.

Parrish, Kyle, "Why Speed to Lead Is Critical for Your Sales Strategy + How to Do It Right," April 19, 2023, https://www.mixmax.com/blog/speed-to-lead.

10

Mapping Your Sales Experience— to Current Customers

YOU HAVE ARRIVED at the last chapter dedicated to the third C, the customized sales journey, and it is a big one. At this stage, intent-based triaging is less important, and organizations are focused on driving adoption, as usage becomes the primary focus. Gartner research reveals that 74% of customers expect more from brands, not only in their products and services but also in how they treat their customers (see the Ramaswami article in the Further Reading section).

An important nuance that many teams miss is that customers' priorities and initiatives can change even after they've purchased a tool or product. In fact, they almost always do. Changes in headcount, the stock market, or other random events can all lead to your main point of contact leaving or a new VP coming in to change things up.

Here are some sobering statics:

- 50% of B2B customers change their priorities within 12 months of purchase (source: Gartner 2022);
- 75% of B2B customers say that their initiatives are constantly evolving (source: McKinsey & Company 2017); and
- 60% of B2B customers say that they are willing to switch vendors if their current vendor does not adapt to their changing needs (source: Salesforce 2023).

When you are designing the sales experience to this stage, you want to make sure that you build processes that capture and address these changes. This is why your customized sales experience cannot end at the contract but instead here at usage.

As mentioned in the last chapter, you may need to build a sales experience that accommodates customers going back to the onboarding stage if they are struggling to adopt the product. You need to map all realistic scenarios that might come up in your customer lifecycle, and this is a very real one. You could even have someone who has been a customer for years but because of the forces of nature mentioned, all of the sudden starts to struggle. It is critical to your organization's success to design your sales experience based on the complete customer lifecycle. How do you handle this currently? Do you have a process built to triage clients who are not using today that isn't dependent on each rep's opinions? Many organizations do not.

As you dive into mapping your sales experience to the initial adoption phase, it will quickly become clear that the way the sales team shows up in the initial and formal evaluation stages affects adoption. Overpromising and poor handoffs to internal team members can prevent buyers from utilizing the full value of your purchase.

% of Customers Who Say Most Companies Treat Them Like a Number

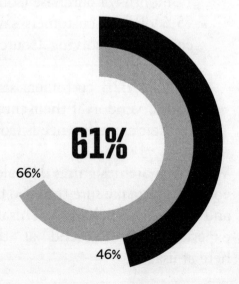

61%

66%

46%

Business buyers   Consumers

61% of customers report feeling "like a number," which provides your company with a major opportunity to differentiate your experience (source: Salesforce 2023). This statistic shows that it is important for businesses to avoid overpromising and to ensure that handoffs to internal team members are smooth and efficient. When businesses overpromise or have poor handoffs, it can lead to customer disappointment and dissatisfaction.

It's not uncommon for companies to go back and add key elements to those stages. That is perfectly fine and encouraged. In fact, the next chapter is dedicated to this mindset, with the fourth C being all about ongoing optimization. The goal now, though, is to build the behaviors that can best lead your customers to power usage, so let's dive in.

The Initial Adoption Stage

The ultimate goal of any company is to turn all its potential clients into power users, and as quickly as possible. Power usage is the ultimate goal of every customer relationship because *that's why the customer actually bought from you!* They bought your product for an outcome, and power usage means they are experiencing its maximum impact and the product or tool has become a part of their new routine. You are now the status quo, which is the goal.

Every company that focuses on getting from initial adoption to power usage will have significantly higher renewal and growth rates. Customers don't want to spend more money or keep spending money if people aren't adopting the product.

From the onboarding stage, you should have established key utilization and usage metrics that signal a client is ready to manage part of the usage on their own. You should have also established a consistent follow-through schedule that ensures that customers stay on track. The goal is to keep customers on this path and move to power usage.

Not every user will become a power user, and that's perfectly okay when dealing with larger sales, but absolutely not okay in small, transactional sales. If one or two or three people aren't using it, you are in trouble.

You will need to map your initial adoption phase, including what you want the initial adoption metrics to look like. The map should show leading indications to power usage. Additionally, you need to think about your sales experience when a customer starts off using your product/solution well but then starts to regress. This will happen more often than not, so you should bake solutions to this problem into your process. You might in fact have to "exit" people back to onboarding-type behavior to ensure they can sustain initial adoption.

Here are a few examples of initial usage metrics and a great graphic to help you think about this process:

- *User acquisition:* The number of new users who signed up or started using the product.
- *Active users:* The number of users who are actively using the product, often categorized as daily active users (DAU), weekly active users (WAU), or monthly active users (MAU).

MEASURE DIGITAL ADOPTION IN 6 STEPS

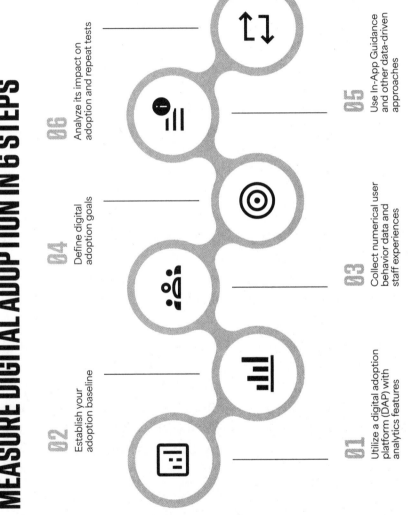

01
Utilize a digital adoption platform (DAP) with analytics features

02
Establish your adoption baseline

03
Collect numerical user behavior data and staff experiences

04
Define digital adoption goals

05
Use In-App Guidance and other data-driven approaches

06
Analyze its impact on adoption and repeat tests

159

- *Retention rate:* The percentage of users who continue to use the product after a certain period of time.
- *Churn rate:* The percentage of users who stop using the product after a certain period of time.
- *User engagement:* How often and how long users are interacting with the product. This can include metrics such as session duration, pages viewed, and features used.
- *Customer satisfaction (CSAT):* A measure of how satisfied users are with the product, often collected through surveys.
- *Net promoter score (NPS):* A measure of how likely users are to recommend the product to others.
- *Conversion rate:* The percentage of users who complete a desired action, such as making a purchase, signing up for a newsletter, or upgrading to a paid plan.
- *Feature adoption:* The percentage of users who are using specific features of the product.
- *Feedback and support tickets:* The number and nature of support tickets or feedback submitted by users.

What's important to establish before your customers move to power usage is the metrics that need to be in place that virtually ensure that a customer won't churn. A power user, by definition, hasn't just adopted the product—it is ingrained into their day-to-day. These metrics will be different for each company, so select only the ones that matter most in your circumstances.

The Power Usage Stage: The Ultimate Goal

This is the goal of every company—to create a product or service that replaces an old way of doing business. You are hitting your KPIs for success, and the client is seeing the maximum benefit from what you provide. If companies can learn to focus on power usage as the ultimate goal of the marketing, sales, and customer success teams, churn will disappear. Customers will be shouting your praises from the rooftop.

Here are some statistics illustrating that power users are extremely valuable to businesses:

- Power users account for 25% of all usage of a product or service, but they generate 75% of the value (source: Gartner 2022).
- Power users are more likely to recommend a product or service to others (source: McKinsey & Company 2017).
- Power users are more likely to become loyal customers and purchase additional products and services from the company (source: Moerkerken 2012).

At this stage, your role is to maintain high usage or utility of your product or service and continue to identify other people that you need to move to power usage or that aren't users but could be. This is all obviously dependent on your sales type, but in almost every sale, the goal is not only to partner with one group or person but to eventually spread and partner with more groups in that company or in the network. Once a customer achieves power usage, as you define it for your company, your goal is to keep them here.

This includes exploring the relationship with your key initial buying group to identify additional areas of support and growth, within their team or outside of it. The key to maintaining this relationship and identifying new potential customers is anchored in the following processes:

- Maintaining a set meeting schedule. Continue meeting and give the customer value-add opportunities at each meeting;
- Usage metrics are met, as defined in the exit criteria in the initial adoption stage; and
- The customer advocates your product/service to others.

When you focus on every customer achieving this criteria, you will enjoy an extremely high renewal rate, receive referrals to new business, and have opportunities to quickly grow your relationship in key accounts. You better assume and believe that no matter how strong your relationship is with the customer, the competition has been in there and at least had an exploratory conversation. So when you are ready to enter the renewal stage, plan ahead and make sure you take no customers for granted. Now is the time when all your work pays off.

The Renewal Process: Mastering the 120-Day Renewal Plan

This is the last step you will typically map to your sales experience. Many companies enter this process too loosely and unstructured. Unlike any other stage in the sales process, the renewal (and to some extent the power-usage) stage should be perpetual. You should view the renewal cycle as a critical component of the customer journey because customers can enter this stage in a good or bad place to renew depending on their experience.

The following section walks you through an easy way to ensure that you renew at the highest possible level. The 120-day renewal plan starts on the first day of signing, and it focuses on constantly staying in the power-usage and growth stage. The goal is to get in front of the renewal early. If you clearly lay out the yearly meeting schedule during the onboarding process, the renewal process will be baked into the plan. The renewal should be a logical extension of an ongoing conversation, instead of a scramble at the last second.

If your client is struggling, this is an opportunity to get them back to the initial adoption or power-usage stages and address the issues. Here are two strategies:

- Determine that they are not a best-fit customer and have a frank conversation with the customer about the issues with usage and the difference between this situation and your best-fit customer situations. Then decide if a renewal even makes sense.
- If they are truly a best-fit customer or they should be based on their needs, agree to put together a mini-POC plan with the customer. This is similar to what you did during the formal evaluation stage. This is a version of the mutual action plan that should help you hard-reset the relationship and solidify the expectations going forward.

Either way, it will be tough to have an easy and successful renewal if you do not establish one of these strategies.

The key to a great renewal is to get it done in a systematized way so the process is clear to the customer. A great renewal process also has a process for getting the client up to speed on features or benefits that they weren't using or that didn't exist when they originally signed.

For the 120-day renewal plan (assuming an annual license), the basics are as follows:

- At the 120-day mark, you conduct a "year in review plan" with your clients and their top initiatives, in relationship to the product purchased, as they see them now for the following year.
- At the 90-day mark, you recap the issues and start to walk through an initial outline of the proposed plan for the following year. You should discuss budget or potential roadblocks to budget here.
- At the 60-day mark, you should spend days 60–90 refining and working through budget with the client and the initial plan for partnership so you can review the final draft 60 days before the renewal date. At this date you should now have a formal proposal that they can work through.
- At the 30-day mark, a contract is in place and should be signed around this time.

One note to point out here is that before the contract being signed, you should *repeat* the exact same steps you did in the onboarding stage by establishing a set meeting schedule in advance. You need to make sure that year two and on go as smoothly as the first year.

Also use this time to assess where your customer might be in their adoption phase and don't hesitate to have a direct conversation about where their usage is compared to other best-fit customers.

The more you focus on onboarding, initial adoption, and power usage, the more the renewal process becomes an outcome of a well-executed process.

Summary

So there you have it: an actual way to work with your customers that is completely driven by what is best for the customers—a sales experience designed with the customers' ideal path in mind, a process that helps customers find the best solution. This solution doesn't just help them with the buying process; it also ensures that the customer has success with the product once they purchase it. The importance of building a sales journey centered on the way your customer wants to buy and has mechanisms in it to triage customers to the right stage of the process quickly is what separates successful and unsuccessful teams.

The next chapter focuses on the fourth C, which is consistent performance optimization. It delves into the mindset of ongoing optimization and explains how sales organizations can more efficiently hit targets. Building your sales experience is just the first step. You have to ensure that you build an experience that optimizes the process on an ongoing basis. Behaviors are changing too quickly for this to be an every few months or years exercise.

Key Takeaways

- **Create a customized sales experience:** It's crucial to understand that customers' priorities can change even after purchase due to various external factors. Design your sales experience to accommodate the entire customer lifecycle, including potential changes to their needs or circumstances.

- **Map the sales experience past the initial sale:** Map it to the initial adoption phase, ensuring that the sales team's actions during the evaluation stages positively affect adoption. Don't overpromise, which can hinder the buyer from realizing the full value of the purchase. Be prepared to revisit and refine your sales experience as you identify areas of improvement.

- **Transition from initial adoption to power usage:** Your ultimate goal should be to transition clients from initial adoption to power usage as quickly as possible. Power usage ensures that customers fully benefit from the product, making it an integral part of their routine. Focus on key metrics that indicate a transition to power usage, thus ensuring that the product becomes ingrained in your customer's day-to-day activities.

- **Maintain power usage:** Regular meetings, monitoring usage metrics, and ensuring the customer advocates for the product are essential strategies for maintaining power usage. Always be on the lookout for opportunities to expand your relationship with key accounts and be prepared for competitive threats.

- **Develop a renewal process:** Create a structured and systematic renewal process, with a clear plan laid out well in advance. Revisit onboarding strategies and assess the customer's current adoption level. I suggest some version of the 120-day process I mentioned above.

Further Reading

Gainsight, "The CS Index 2022," https://www.gainsight.com/benchmarks/customer-success-index-2022-tool/.

Gartner, "Gartner Glossary: Customer Success," https://www.gartner.com/en/sales/glossary/customer-success.

Gartner, "Gartner Identifies Top Five Trends in Privacy through 2024," May 31, 2022, https://www.gartner.com/en/newsroom/press-releases/2022-05-31-gartner-identifies-top-five-trends-in-privacy-through-2024.

McKinsey & Company, "The People Power of Transformations," 2017, https://www.mckinsey.com/~/media/mckinsey/business%20functions/people%20and%20organizational%20performance/our%20insights/the%20people%20power%20of%20transformations/the-people-power-of-transformations.pdf.

McKinsey, "McKinsey Global Institute," April 6, 2022, https://www.mckinsey.com/mgi/overview.

Moerkerken, Jochem, Kim Petrick, Andreas Dullweber, and Barney Hamilton, "Turning on Utility Customer Loyalty," Bain & Company, November 6, 2012, https://www.bain.com/insights/turning-on-utility-customer-loyalty/.

Ovington, Tristan, "How to Measure & Track Digital Adoption with KPIs & Metrics," May 9, 2023, https://www.digital-adoption.com/digital-adoption-metrics/.

Ramaswami, Rama, "Brand Strategies Focused on Dependability Score Highest on Customer Trust," Gartner, December 1, 2020, https://www.gartner.com/en/marketing/insights/articles/brand-strategies-focused-dependability-score-highest.

Salesforce, "State of the Connected Customer, 6th Edition," 2023, https://www.salesforce.com/resources/research-reports/state-of-the-connected-customer/.

11

The Fourth C: Consistent Performance Optimization

IT'S TIME TO dive into the fourth C, which is *consistent performance optimization*. Many B2B sales organizations do not have a consistent process in place to optimize their sales experience from pipeline generation through the renewal process. This chapter gives you a road map that can make this process approachable and easy to execute with the team you have today. If you are a sales rep, then this mindset is applicable to you as well. Every rep and every organization must have a process in place to optimize their sales results at each step of the process.

Why does this matter? Let's do the math. Say that ABC corporation is trying to find ways to generate more meetings. Their team decides they need to redo their outbound process because the results just aren't where they need to be. The sales managers have been asking the team to do more activities, run contests, and try to motivate the team to get out more emails and calls, but the numbers still aren't producing the results needed. The managers have come to the realization that the "more" button isn't going to get it done and decide they need to optimize the strategy as a whole.

They do a big eight-week sprint to rewrite the sequences and upgrade the call track. They see a 10% increase in results. They are excited by the results and continue to run the new play for the year. The results still aren't where they would like, but the increase is promising. This is how 90% of our clients operate initially.

Now let's compare that to more innovative organizations. These teams also aren't where they want to be, but they take a different approach. Instead of doing a big overhaul, they decide to set up better reporting to see which parts have been successful, and then they make two or three adjustments to the sequences with good initial results—a 3% increase. They also realize that if they don't set up a process for ongoing optimization, they may not see the results that they all know are possible. So they run this process once every few weeks. By the end of the year, that 3% monthly increase in performance leads to an approximately 143% increase in performance after 12 months. Instead of doing big, grand overhauls every 12 months that might get better results initially, the team that implements small, consistent improvements over shorter periods will see much bigger results in the long run. This is why consistent optimization isn't an option—it's the only path forward.

This last C has three pillars, each discussed in this chapter:

- Measure what matters most;
- Have a process for execution; and
- Moonshots.

There are a million metrics that you can look to optimize, but the first pillar of this last C focuses on a few critical metrics where small changes made on a regular basis lead to the biggest impact.

Pillar One: Measure What Matters Most

There are hundreds or maybe even thousands of metrics a sales organization could track, and many times I feel as though analysts just track and report on numbers for the sake of reporting. It feels good to track activities and watch dials, but at the end of the day there are very few metrics that actually move the needle for your organization. Teams that make consistent optimizations on only the most important metrics will see much greater results than the overly busy teams hell-bent on tracking everything.

First, let's consider some of the key metrics that will move the needle and generate new leads. There may be other metrics for your business, but these are the most consistent I've seen work quickly when they're optimized regularly.

Inbound Lead Metrics

- Time to follow up from sales team to lead;
- Time to book meeting from inbound inquiry;
- Quality lead versus unqualified lead ratio; and
- Landing page conversion rate to quality lead.

Outbound Opportunity Metrics

- Positive reply rates to emails or calls;
- Sequence step that is top performing (for example, out of the eight touchpoints in the process, step 4 is working best);
- Type of content with the highest conversion rate (emails/videos/calls/LinkedIn messages);
- Opportunities generated;
- New meetings run; and
- Meeting show rate.

What you don't see here are things such as open rates, replies, and even website traffic. It's not that those metrics aren't something to look at, but they don't let you optimize quickly.

They are interesting metrics but don't lead to direct results. The key to keep in mind is not to track a bunch of metrics, do big overhauls, and think you need to make big waves to see results. Optimizing one of these data points consistently can lead to major results.

You can find full definitions of all of these metrics at resources .innovativesellerbook.com.

Sales Experience Metrics

- Sales cycle at each stage; and
- Stage conversion rate at each stage.

These two are my favorites. There are others that you can track for team performance and forecasting, but when it comes to consistent metrics that you can look at to optimize your sales experience, these are the most critical. When you understand *stage velocity*, the speed at which someone moves from each stage to the next, at the macro, team, and individual level, it can be easy to see where a rep or team is struggling.

For example, if a rep has a short sales cycle in the first two parts of the process but then a long "trial" stage, they may be struggling to set clear metrics for success in the trial. If teams are struggling because a stage is taking a long time, then you may need to rewrite your playbook for just that stage. Conversion rates have the same concept. When you break them down by stage, you can see the bottlenecks in the process. Maybe it's poor questions you are asking, and you need to look at the playbook and adjust. Maybe the proposal process has a low conversion rate, so you need to fix that stage.

The key to this mindset and these metrics is that you aren't looking at doing big playbook overhauls every two to three years. Instead, you're making small improvements to the sales process monthly/quarterly. This Agile method will lead to much faster iterations and results than the typical big waterfall-style release mindset. The data will tell you how to continue fixing bottlenecks and increasing your deal velocity to drive better speed and efficiency in your sales experience.

Client Retention and Growth Metrics

When it comes to optimizing your work with your current customers, the numbers here are also pretty straightforward. Power usage is always the goal, so you want to make sure that you have metrics in place to track customer usage, review them regularly, and have a process to triage customers who are struggling.

You probably already set your customer metrics when you went through the onboarding and initial adoption parts, because power usage is so important. Here are those KPIs from the last chapter. Remember, you can track all of them, but only a certain few are good to optimize. Don't try to track everything to the detriment of focusing your team and time on what matters most.

- *Active users:* The number of users who are actively using the product, often categorized as daily active users (DAU), weekly active users (WAU), and monthly active users (MAU).
- *Retention rate:* The percentage of users who continue to use the product after a certain period of time.

- *Churn rate:* The percentage of users who stop using the product after a certain period of time.
- *User engagement:* How often and how long users are interacting with the product. This can include metrics such as session duration, pages viewed, and features used.
- *Customer satisfaction (CSAT):* A measure of how satisfied users are with the product, often collected through surveys.
- *Net promoter score (NPS):* A measure of how likely users are to recommend the product to others.
- *Conversion rate:* The percentage of users who complete a desired action, such as making a purchase, signing up for a newsletter, or upgrading to a paid plan.
- *Feature adoption:* The percentage of users who are using specific features of the product.
- *Feedback and support tickets:* The number and nature of support tickets or feedback submitted by users.

Many companies overfocus on using product training to solve problems, when the bigger issue is an internal blocker or people reverting to old habits. Make sure when you are designing your sales experience and then your optimization plan that you have metrics in place and strategies to match that solve change management problems. Active user metrics are usually a good indicator, but then how do you address the lack of usage outside of more training?

For each of these three components of your sales experience, try to limit yourself to the two to four metrics that matter most. Now that you have your KPIs to track, you have to build in a process to do something about them. You have to be able to make changes to the sales experience based on results and trends quickly and not in the traditional "big overhaul" way.

Pillar Two: Have a Process for Execution

I boiled down all sales challenges as process problems in earlier chapters so if you want to build a culture of "always optimizing," then you need to nail the process first and supplement it with the right people and technology. It is important to not limit your thinking. Avoid excuses such as "We don't have time," "We don't have the people," "Who is going to own . . .?" because you won't design the optimal process. This is why I see countless teams struggle to implement a solid, consistent optimization plan. They limit what they think they can do before they even start.

There are three key areas for every organization to address to create this always-optimizing culture and mindset in their teams. The following examples address for outbound optimization, but the same three areas need to be addressed when you build the process for optimizing your sales process and work with your current customers. You should build the exact same process for optimizing your sales process and customer engagement process.

Example Outbound Optimization Process

Consider this example outbound optimization process, which you can tweak as needed for your own use:

1. *Establish your review schedule:* If you are pumping more than 100,000 activities through a system, you should be looking at this and adjusting every two weeks.

Bigger teams should be doing it weekly. This scheduled meeting should review the following:

- Sequence success review charts;
- Specific content review insights;
- Week-over-week changes to top-performing sequences; and
- Economic trends that you need to be prepared for in order to adjust the copywriting schedule.

2. *Establish the team:* Do you have someone internally who is an expert at data review, copywriting, and strategic optimization? The reality is that most teams do not, so they need to look for an agency to support them—Skaled is leading the way in this space—or make sure the internal team clearly defines each of these roles. Think of this as an investment and not a cost center. There is a reason your marketing team pays an agency 10%–20% of their ad spend to optimize it. It's an investment that generates improved results.

- *Data and insights lead:* This person is responsible for pulling the data on a weekly/biweekly basis and then providing insights into what sequences are working and which pieces of content are working the best and then producing recommendations for ways to update sequences. You also need to make sure that you periodically review what isn't working systematically and sunset those approaches.
- *Strategic lead:* This is someone who is responsible for reviewing the data and insights and then making new changes to the sequences every two weeks.

They need to be experts in Outreach or similar tools and not just admins; they need to know what is possible.

- *Content/copywriter*: This person is responsible for writing new copy across cold call scripts, emails, LinkedIn, gifting, and other platforms.

3. *Develop a governance process for reps to try new experiments and innovation:* Sequence optimization should never be siloed to one team. Every organization needs a process where reps can have that 10% of freedom to try new things. Then when those things work, the data and insights team can look to replicate across the organization.

If you want to build an organization that is focused on optimization, you need to have all three of these components. It's amazing to see what can happen when you build an innovation and performance mindset into your organization. You teams will be happier, and results happen much faster.

It is critical that you rinse and repeat this optimization plan for your sales process as well—you have to build a similar optimization process for your sales organization and process. Completely disregard the old way of paying certain Command or Big 4 consulting firms to redo your sales process every three years and instead, you have to optimize every few months. Your sales organization needs to be able to take cues from modern customer behaviors and adapt in real time.

So now that you've read how to master the process of optimization and ensure that your team is set up for success for years to come, you're ready to consider how to incorporate big leaps into your organization's optimization cycle. Small optimization is the most critical path to hitting your results, but moonshots can take you to places you never thought possible.

Pillar Three: Moonshots

The term *moonshot* originates from the ambitious space missions undertaken by NASA, specifically the Apollo program that aimed to land humans on the Moon and bring them safely back to Earth. The most famous of these missions was Apollo 11 in 1969, when astronauts Neil Armstrong and Buzz Aldrin became the first humans to walk on the Moon.

A moonshot represents a goal that is incredibly challenging, requires significant resources and innovation, and is not guaranteed to succeed.

Over time, the term has been adopted in the business and technology sectors to describe ambitious, groundbreaking projects that aim to achieve something that's currently believed to be nearly impossible. Moonshot projects often require radical thinking and approaches that differ from the status quo. In the modern context, a moonshot project is one that aims to solve a massive problem.

When sales organizations aspire to generate more leads or close more deals, they often turn to producing more activities rather than improving the quality of the process. I've talked about this enough now, hopefully, but I haven't talked about how this is stifling innovation. You might lose opportunities not because you lack creativity and innovation but because you don't give your organization time to actually innovate.

This emphasis on dedicated innovation time is supported by real evidence. For example, a study by Boston Consulting Group found that companies that dedicated innovation time for employees were 2.8 times more likely to have high rates of innovation than companies that did not (source: Manly et al. 2023). The study also found that companies with strong innovation cultures had 19% higher revenue growth than companies with weaker innovation cultures.

Instead of asking salespeople to be more creative and "break the system" to generate 20, 30, or 40 meetings or increase their close rate by 20%, we are managing metrics that are the averages of good, bad, okay, and great performers. We are focused on what's easy to track and measure without any room for big swings that may be more difficult to measure over time but yield far superior results. The revenue results are real. Companies that are innovators have a much larger market cap then their peers—nearly 120% higher. Moonshots aren't just about keeping people engaged; they're about driving revenue as well.

Your organization as a whole should be engaged in creative innovation throughout the process. This begins with investing more in research to continuously improve. Who is the real buyer? Have you polled 20, 30, or 40 of them to confirm that they care about this message? Where do they live? Have

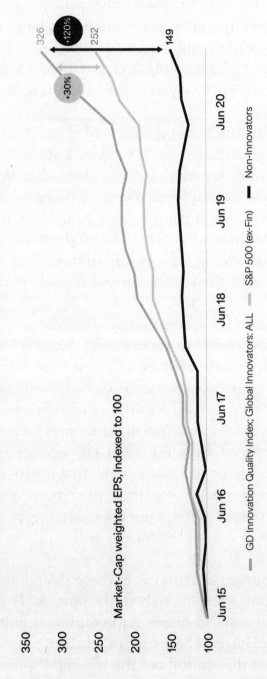

24-MONTH FORWARD EARNINGS

All Innovators 120% higher compared to Non-Innovators

Market-Cap weighted EPS, Indexed to 100

350
300
250
200
150
100

Jun 15 Jun 16 Jun 17 Jun 18 Jun 19 Jun 20

326 +120%
252
149

+30%

GD Innovation Quality Index: Global Innovators: ALL
S&P 500 (ex-Fin)
Non-Innovators

you polled 20, 30, or 40 of them to confirm they are at their desk, in the field, at trade shows, or on LinkedIn? If you want to double, triple, or quadruple sales results, the answer can't just be to "do more." With a consistent optimization plan that bakes in time for moonshots, you will achieve amazing improvements in your sales results. This is the same for the sales process. How are you encouraging your team to create better experiences for your clients as well? The innovations can't always come from the top. There needs to be a way for sales reps and leaders to feed innovative ideas up the ladder as well.

Here are five ideas to get you started:

- Make sure every seller has two to three hours per week dedicated to reviewing what's working to see what they can optimize.
- Make sure every seller has time dedicated to write or experiment on calls.
- Build in a monthly meeting to review results, and have teams brainstorm new ideas.
- The executive team should meet for a half day each quarter to look at the various bottlenecks in the process and assign team leads to develop possible solutions.
- Relax some of the governance settings on your top performers, tools to allow them more freedom in what they do and track so they have more time to innovate.

Summary

I could—and who knows, maybe will—write an entire book just on this topic. There is a reason it is one of the 4 Cs to innovative selling, and it's interesting how we see the results of compounded small gains in many parts of our life, from our 401(k) to working out: when we invest in consistent improvement, we see the results in time.

When you build an amazing sales experience, it's important to understand that it probably isn't perfect the first time it's deployed and, moreover, will never be perfect. You and your team will invest a good amount of time mapping your sales experience, but you still have to look at that at step zero. That is the kickoff. The team needs to have a consistent optimization plan in place to see big results. If not, you will be the 10% improved team who thinks they made a dent but left massive results on the table because they moved on to the next thing. Your sales experience is a living and breathing part of your organization. It can't be put in the corner and inspected annually; it needs a small amount of water regularly to truly blossom.

Key Takeaways

- **Develop a consistent optimization mindset:** Small, regular improvements yield better long-term results than infrequent overhauls. This is applicable to your sales reps and your organization as a whole. Encourage your team to embrace this mindset in their daily activities, fostering a culture where continuous improvement is the norm rather than the exception.
- **Focus on valuable metrics:** Not all metrics are equally valuable; it's essential to concentrate on ones that genuinely affect results. Metrics such as time to follow up, sequence step performance, and stage conversion rates

are more actionable than mere open rates or website traffic. Prioritize metrics that offer insights into customer behaviors and preferences, as these will guide more effective sales strategies.

- **Create a structured process:** A successful optimization culture requires a clear review schedule, defined team roles, and a governance process for innovation. Sales issues often boil down to process issues. Implementing a structured process ensures consistency and accountability, making it easier to identify areas for improvement.
- **Set ambitious goals (moonshots):** Ambitious goals drive innovation, so allocate time for innovation, allowing for ambitious goals that lead to significant advancements. These goals inspire teams to push beyond their comfort zones and achieve extraordinary results.
- **Be innovative:** Encourage "play" and experimentation to find creative solutions and improved results. Don't focus solely on quantity. Fostering an environment where creativity is valued can lead to breakthrough ideas and strategies that set your sales process apart.
- **Treat sales as a continuous journey:** You must regularly nurture and update your sales process. Initially deploying your sales experience is just the beginning. Continuous refinement and adaptation to market changes and customer feedback are crucial for sustained success.

Further Reading

Manly, Justin, Michael Ringel, Amy MacDougall, Will Cornock, Johann D. Harnoss, Konstantinos Apostolatos, Ramón Baeza, Ryoji Kimura, Michael Ward, Beth Viner,

Jean-Manuel Izaret, Wendi Backler, Vladimir Lukic, Sylvain Duranton, and Romain de Laubier, "Reaching New Heights in Uncertain Times," Boston Consulting Group, May 23, 2022, https://www.bcg.com/publications/2023/advantages-through-innovation-in-uncertain-times.

Miller, Serena, "10 Strategies to Build a Successful Cross-Functional Team," Outreach.io, June 7, 2022, https://www.outreach.io/resources/blog/cross-functional-team-best-practices.

Pipelineapp.io, "75% of Cross-Functional Teams Are Dysfunciontal," March 31, 2023, https://www.pipelineapp.io/resources/news-insights/75-percent-cross-functional-teams-dysfunctional/.

12

The Future of Sales: *Generative AI* and the Changing Role of Sales

My HOPE IS that after each chapter, you paused, took action, and now have it all figured out. If that's not the case, don't worry, because you have all the tools you need to turn your sales experience into an innovative one that is customer first.

The concepts of the 4 Cs typically exist in most revenue organizations today, but many groups are too busy or siloed to have an impact. We are picking up too many new projects, marking projects that are getting up and running complete prematurely, and not coordinating across groups—duplicating and recreating work already handled. If you focus on each of the Cs together and across departments, the change you see will be remarkable. If you are an Innovative Seller as rep, then you can start to implement most of these principles as well on your own.

While coming up with the concepts in the 4 Cs, I was primarily focused on creating a process that can withstand a world that is evolving rapidly. Technology, AI, consumer preferences, and employment preferences are all rapidly changing, The 4 Cs can help to serve as a guide that you can consult throughout your own journey and evolution as a seller, no matter what the market throws at you. There are a few trends I want to leave you with that by the time this book is published will be at the forefront of your daily life already or in the near future. That is the rise of *Generative AI* and the role of the seller in the loop in years to come.

What ChatGPT Means for You Now and Tomorrow

My best estimation is that by 2025, whether it is ChatGPT or something similar, nearly every seller will have a *Generative AI* copilot. When you access resources.innovativesellerbook .com you will get access to Javin, which is the future of bringing your playbook to life with an LLM such as ChatGPT. I recently led the course for LinkedIn Learning on ChatGPT for sales that launched in late 2023, so I won't get into every use case for ChatGPT, but this chapter does highlight why every sales organization needs to have a strategy for implementing right now in key areas of the process. Executives in particular are working to integrate this throughout their business with nearly 80% saying they are embracing *Generative AI*. For my sales leaders, it's going to be critical.

MY COMPANY IS EMBRACING *GENERATIVE AI*

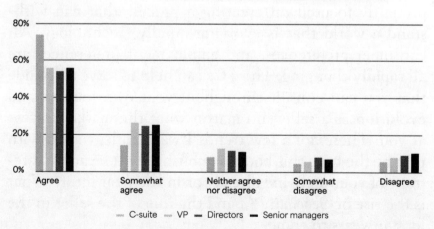

Let me talk you straightforwardly through two key ways for organizations to embrace ChatGPT to drive more leads and sales. I've spent hundreds of hours reviewing these strategies and have distilled some of my best practices here.

Pipeline Generation

This section looks at three key ways to use ChatGPT for preparation and research: general training, individual research, and company research.

General training involves getting teams up to speed on the buyer persona they sell to. You can use a setting in ChatGPT called Custom Instructions to teach ChatGPT whom you sell to, what they care about, and where you fit in the ecosystem. Your team can then ask ChatGPT questions about the persona you sell to in an industry to make sure they can write better messaging. This general training use case is amazing at helping companies get salespeople up to speed on trends and buyer preferences so they can have higher-quality conversations faster. We are actively training and conducting workshops on how to do this for your own organization when you visit the resources page.

Next ChatGPT can help research individuals. You can paste in a LinkedIn profile or give ChatGPT a link to someone's blog and ask it to summarize the person's communication style or their work history. Imagine condensing three or four Google searches, LinkedIn research, and pondering what might be relevant to this individual from hours to minutes. It's not just about saving time; it also raises the quality of the touchpoints to another level.

You can apply the same logic to company research. Imagine feeding ChatGPT an entire annual report and then asking for areas where your product might be able to help. It's a tremendous opportunity to save yourself and your team hours a year, and the research quality is also high. You can feed it the company's investor relations page, your product page, and then ask ChatGPT to highlight current happenings at the company that may be relevant to what you can offer. The opportunity here is limitless. You can truly supercharge your research efforts and have executive-level conversations with just minutes of research.

The good news is that you don't need to be an expert at using ChatGPT. I've listed all of our top prompts at resources .innovativesellerbook.com for prep and research. Feel free to use and share them freely.

Next, you can apply all of that research to writing amazing messaging to help generate more pipeline leads. I've seen hundreds of new companies that promise better messaging with AI, but tools such as ChatGPT do an amazing job out of the box. When you take the information you find from research and then ask ChatGPT or tools like it to write concise messaging, the results are fantastic. You can take messaging a step further by feeding it examples of someone's writing style and then have it customize the message based on how that person prefers to communicate. You can paste in their LinkedIn profile and have it summarize their experience to then use in a cold call or personalized video. The ability to compile insights about someone and turn that into effective messaging is the future of personalization and how people will achieve pipeline goals in years to come. If you want a more contained and customized experience for your specific sales organization, that's where Javin comes in, so feel free to reach out on the site and learn more.

I hope that this leads to much higher quality messaging coming from teams for outreach and a shift away from the bulk spam we see today. There is no reason to send bulk spam when high-quality insights are so easy to find and apply to amazing messaging.

Closing More Deals

Generative AI tools are also extremely helpful in the sales process itself. They can help salespeople play out scenarios in advance and close more deals because they can come up with the right solution more often. Here are two strategies for prompting that can change the way your team sells and the way managers coach their teams.

The following example is a scenario-based prompt to help you close a deal. You need to make sure you are using a *Generative AI* tool that can access current websites for this:

My company, (link), has had two meetings with a VP of sales.

In the first meeting he highlighted two issues.

1. [issue 1]
2. [issue 2]

He had some interest, specifically (insert product page link). We now have meetings with the CRO, who may care about a slow-down in outbound sales and overall cost, and the IT director, who at times can be a blocker because of past tech migration failures and possible unforeseen costs that rarely get budgeted. Based on this, help me to write a meeting structure that will address key concerns and eliminate objections before they come up.

The result includes advice to tactfully address objections from the client and how to acknowledge their concerns, offer solutions, and emphasize the value of your product or service. The time savings and quality of conversations that result from this type of prompting are fantastic.

Another prompt strategy for sales reps and teams is to improve specific sales skills. One of the biggest barriers for salespeople achieving the highest level of sales is continuous professional development. This is an area in which Chat-GPT excels.

Here is an example:

I have a meeting coming up with a Fortune 500 VP of operations, and I'm not sure how communicating with her might be different than a meeting I have with someone at the director level. Typically the director level cares about their team seeing value in how our team saves them time by automating back office ordering. Based on trends in manufacturing today and the difference in roles, what should I focus on with the VP versus director?

The result of this prompt can help you elevate your conversation to an executive level and keep executives engaged throughout the process. It can potentially save reps years of on-the-fly learning by allowing them to improve almost any skill in real time.

These two prompt strategies can help sellers close more deals, as they now can plan for almost any sales scenario in advance. Every sales organization can leverage ChatGPT with its own scenarios and see how it can quickly have a big impact on driving more sales for the organization.

There are many more applications for *Generative AI* in sales. Our team at Skaled has built a tool where you can upload your own playbook to leverage all of the insights here from *Innovative Selling* to fill in the gaps, and then allow reps to quickly access their own best practices. It leverages the *generative AI* to make discovery of best practices and scenario planning easy and bakes in your specific buyer and products as well. This tool is truly revolutionary in bringing organizations, and sales leaders, best practices to life to ensure the sales team can execute effectively at each step of the sales process.

Generative AI tools will certainly help sales organizations better communicate with new and existing customers, but it's only one part of the story. As you've read throughout this book, how a company sells is one part of the equation. Changes in consumer behavior are the ultimate driving force behind the need for new innovative selling strategies.

The Shifting Role of the Salesperson

As *Generative AI* and other tools become the day-to-day sales experience and consumers continue to shift their behaviors, knowing when and how to have the sales team and other service teams in the loop will be a critical part of journey for years to come.

According to Gartner's projection on B2B sales interactions:

- By 2025, 80% of B2B sales interactions between suppliers and buyers will occur through digital channels.
- 33% of all buyers desire a seller-free sales experience, a preference that rises to 44% for Millennials.
- Buyers typically spend only 17% of their time meeting with potential suppliers when considering a purchase.
- Sales reps will need to embrace new tools and channels to align their sales activity with customers' buying practices and information collecting needs.

You've already mapped the areas for your sales organization where you want to allow people to self-guide or learn asynchronously, which is a great start. Our world is changing rapidly, though. Remember the fourth C (continuous performance optimization)—our world and the place for the salesperson in that experience will evolve rapidly as well. Here are the two key areas I see sales reps staying relevant and influential in the process for years to come. If you are looking at the skills to build or to train your team, these are the two that matter most to the modern buyer.

The Future of Salespeople in the Loop

First, reps will be required to be experts in the field they sell to and understand creative ways to help buyers solve challenges. If they can't do these two areas of sales well, the likelihood a buyer will want to interact with a seller will continue to diminish. 60% of sellers say they always put the buyer first, but only 24% of buyers agree (source: Calnan 2021).

I can already see sellers asking, "But what about building a relationship with the buyer? That is critical to sales." I get it, and actually I am saying the same thing. Buyers want to self-guide and learn more on their own, so the ability to build trust when a buyer does reach out to a salesperson will be critical. Buyers are going to be looking for those first few sales interactions that provide real value.

McKinsey highlights this well in one of their latest reports, where 70%–80% of buyers wanted a remote or self-service experience. This doesn't mean that they don't want a human interaction; it's that they also want a strong digital interaction.

% of B2B Decision-Makers Who Prefer Remote Human Interactions Or Digital Self-Service

~70-80%

The human part of relationships will be important as always, but this has to be balanced with conversations that have substance. Additionally, skills such as creativity will be at a premium when it comes to sales and buyer interactions.

Buyers can access the basics themselves. They can look at a demo, think through how it might help them, talk to a few peers, and read reviews from other buyers. When they are ready to move to the next step, they want to talk to a salesperson to come up with the perfect solution for their use case. They won't want a tone-deaf demo that repeats what they already know. They won't want to be asked the same questions over and over again. They won't want to have pricing held back or to be qualified.

They want a salesperson who can creatively match their unique situation. Sales reps in the future will have to add value and create unique solutions for clients because buyers can find the basic fit on their own. Added value has to come in the form of expertise and creativity. The good news is that *Generative AI* and various specialized sales tools can help sales reps get up to speed quickly and come up with creative solutions more easily. These tools can help salespeople have more productive conversations immediately and get up to speed on new situations quickly to provide the best solutions for their buyers.

Salespeople as Experts of the Ecosystem

Next, sellers will need to be an expert of the ecosystem their product lives in and other solutions that both compete with and complement their offering. Buyers are reviewing reports from Gartner, Forrester, and many research sites to learn how products fit into the ecosystem of other tools and products as well. With all this access to third-party insights and information, sellers must have similar knowledge as the buyer. Sellers who cannot articulate and differentiate their service or product will struggle to see success in this vetted and educated buyer world. If a seller must rely on a sales engineer or someone else on the team to be the person who can get a customer an answer, then the customer will want to skip many of those interactions altogether and just talk to people who can add value. They are asking their friends in Teams and Slack the best solution, so sellers need to know what is being said and matters to buyers.

I am hopeful that more and more companies will invest more time in their onboarding process and in continual training to keep their teams up to speed. My fear is that too many sales organizations continue to focus on their own process and the way they want to sell, and they don't spend enough time understanding the ecosystem and learn how to help a customer make the right, integrated decision. This lack of understanding is one of the biggest reasons that sellers lose deals to the status quo. The buyer never fully understands how the product differentiates from what they are doing and how it will complement their broader ecosystem of tools or services they use today.

The salesperson must have the same, if not more, education on the competitive landscape and ecosystem or buyers will continue to opt for more self-service options. After all, if the buyer already has more information than the person they are talking to, why would they deal with a salesperson at all?

I do strongly believe that self-service buying in B2B will continue to become more popular for increasingly bigger-ticket items. Organizations will have to make sure they have this option to buy with credit card or PO online, while maintaining a strong onboarding process for buyers so that vetted buyers can just purchase, and the salesperson or success manager will come in to the picture after the sale. We shouldn't fear this motion, as the salesperson will still need to be in the loop. It's just a matter of determining the right time to step in. If the salesperson isn't adding exceptional service, buyers will work with organizations that have sales teams that are trained well. If not, they will look to self-guide.

Wrapping It Up

Never fear, as the salesperson will remain a key part of the sales process for decades to come. Selling after all is not information giving. It's helping to guide someone to the right decision and highlighting the uniqueness of your product along the way so they buy. As I wrap up this chapter and book, my hope is that you see this new world coming for B2B sales and embrace these changes the same way you embraced shifts in how customers buy online.

Sales organizations that can adapt to this new world will thrive. They will provide unique and differentiated experiences for their buyers, and new customers will flock to these companies for their innovation. Now is the time to embrace a customized sales process to avoid becoming the B2B Blockbuster. Now is the time to get in front of the pack and build a sales journey that embraces the 4 Cs and creates customized journeys for buyers based on the buyer's preferences. In ten years, my guess is that we will see a case study written about a big, industry-leading B2B company that was brought down by its competitors—not because of a superior product but because the giant organization stuck with the "rent in store" model. They stuck with MEDDIC or other BANT or other processes that fit the sales organization but were archaic to the buyer. Companies cannot continue to look backward for strategies to innovate their sales processes; they must look forward. The future is here, and it will be fun and exciting for sellers and buyers as we create new ways to build relationships—with technology and humans at the forefront.

Key Takeaways

- **Embrace *Generative AI* and ChatGPT:** Using AI-powered tools (e.g. chatbots) for lead generation has been shown to lead to higher conversion rates. You can also ask ChatGPT questions about your customers and to write better messaging to them. *Generative AI* tools can also help you play out scenarios in advance and close more deals because they can come up with the right solution more often.
- **Prepare for the changing role of the salesperson:** Sales reps in the future will have to add value and create unique solutions for clients, because buyers can find the basic information on their own. Added value comes in the form of expertise and creativity. Salespeople must be more educated on the competitive landscape and ecosystem, or buyers will continue to opt for self-service options.
- **Provide more:** Companies that succeed in the new world of AI-generated sales have to provide unique and differentiated experiences for their buyers. If you can do that well, new customers will flock to your company for its innovation.

Further Reading

Bages-Amat, Arnau, Liz Harrison, Dennis Spillecke, and Jennifer Stanley, "These Eight Charts Show How COVID-19 Has Changed B2B Sales Forever," McKinsey & Company, October 14, 2020, https://www.mckinsey.com/capabilities/growth-marketing-and-sales/our-insights/these-eight-charts-show-how-covid-19-has-changed-b2b-sales-forever.

"DemandWorks Media," https://www.dwmedia.com/demandthatworks/.

Fisher, Brittany Furnari, "Revolutionizing Lead Generation: How ChatGPT Could Change the Game," LinkedIn Sales Solutions, 2023, https://www.linkedin.com/pulse/revolutionizing-lead-generation-how-chatgpt-could-brittany/.

Gartner, "Gartner Says 80% of B2B Sales Interactions between Suppliers and Buyers Will Occur in Digital Channels by 2025," September 15, 2020, https://www.gartner.com/en/newsroom/press-releases/2020-09-15-gartner-says-80--of-b2b-sales-interactions-between-su.

Lindenau, Kelly, "Demand Gen Report," April 28, 2020, https://www.demandgenreport.com/.

Index

203